Anonymous

Final Report of the Proceedings of the Masonic Board of Relief of the City of Chicago

Anonymous

Final Report of the Proceedings of the Masonic Board of Relief of the City of Chicago

ISBN/EAN: 9783744692342

Printed in Europe, USA, Canada, Australia, Japan

Cover: Foto ©ninafisch / pixelio.de

More available books at **www.hansebooks.com**

FINAL REPORT

OF THE

PROCEEDINGS

OF THE

Masonic Board of Relief,

OF THE

CITY OF CHICAGO,

ORGANIZED

TO DISTRIBUTE THE FUNDS AND OTHER AID SENT FROM ABROAD
FOR THE RELIEF OF MASTER MASONS, AND THE WIDOWS
AND CHILDREN OF DECEASED BRETHREN, WHO
WERE RENDERED NEEDY BY THE GREAT
CONFLAGRATION IN THE CITY
OF CHICAGO, OCTOBER
8TH AND 9TH,
A. D. 1871.

CHICAGO:

HAZLITT & REED, PRINTERS, 139 AND 141 MONROE STREET.

1872.

TO THE ANCIENT AND HONORABLE FRATERNITY OF FREE AND ACCEPTED MASONS THROUGHOUT THE UNITED STATES, CANADA, AND ELSEWHERE, WHOSE FRATERNAL KINDNESS AND SPONTANEOUS GENROSITY SO GREATLY ASSUAGED THE MISFORTUNE AND DISTRESS OF THEIR BRETHREN, AS WELL AS THE WIDOWS AND ORPHANS OF DECEASED MASONS, WHO WERE RENDERED NEEDY BY THE AWFUL CALAMITY OF THE EVER MEMORABLE EIGHTH AND NINTH OF OCTOBER, 1871, THIS REPORT IS GRATEFULLY AND AFFECTIONATELY SUBMITTED.

FINAL REPORT

OF THE

Masonic Board of Relief.

The recent great conflagration which laid waste and destroyed the fairest portion of the city of Chicago, included in its ravages the total destruction of a number of beautiful Halls, together with the Charters, Records, Jewels, Paraphrenalia and other property, of eighteen Lodges, two Chapters, one Council, two Commanderies, and the four co-ordinate bodies of the A. & A. Scottish Rite, viz :

Oriental	Lodge,	No.	33, (lost Hall,)
Garden City	"	"	141,
Waubansia	"	"	160,
Germania	"	"	182,
Wm. B. Warren	"	"	209,
Blaney	"	"	271, (lost Hall,)
Accordia	"	"	277,
Ashlar	"	"	308,
Dearborn	"	"	310,
Kilwinning	"	"	311, (lost Hall,)
Blair	"	"	393, (lost Hall,)
Thos. J. Turner	"	"	409,
Mithra	"	"	410, (lost Hall,)
Chicago	"	"	437,
H. W. Bigelow	"	"	438,
Covenant	"	"	526, (lost Hall,)
Lincoln Park	"	"	611, (lost Hall,)
Keystone	"	"	639,

LaFayette Chapter, R. A. M., No. 2,
Corinthian   "   "   " 69,
Chicago Council, R. & S. M., No. 4,
Grand Council of State of Illinois,
Apollo Commandery, No. 1, K. T., (lost Hall,)
St. Bernard Commandery, No. 35, K. T., ⁃
Van Rensselaer G. L. of Perfection, A. & A. Scottish Rite,
Chicago Council Princes of Jerusalem,   "   "
Gourgas Chapter Rose Croix,   "   "
Oriental Sovereign Consistory,   "   "
And the entire contents of the M. W. Grand Master's office.

Thus, in a few hours, the craft of our city was reduced from a condition of comparative affluance and comfort, to that of poverty and distress.

TEMPORARY ORGANIZATION OF RELIEF COMMITTEE.

On Thursday, October 12th, a few brethren convened at Masonic Temple, in the West Division, and organized as a committee, for the purpose of relieving those of the fraternity who were then suffering by reason of the fire.

Such was the tumult and confusion consequent upon the appalling disaster, that it was a matter of great difficulty for friends to find, or communicate with each other. However, this little band of Brothers commenced the good work with, at this time, but scanty means to supply the wants of the needy.

Upon application to the Louisville Relief Committee, who had already established a depot of supplies in the city, and to the Mayor and others, in charge of provisions and clothing sent hither by a generous world, they promptly responded, by placing at the disposal of our committee sufficient to meet the immediate demands upon them.

But at this moment, the noble craft, everywhere, was at labor in behalf of their distressed brethren, and but a few hours elapsed before the "mystic current" was flashed through the wires, from East, West, South, yea, and from the "*North*," conveying the glad tidings that succor was at hand.

The unexampled outpouring of Masonic charity which ensued, was indeed commensurate with the awful necessity. Liberal donations were received from all quarters, by telegram, by letter, and by individual brethren; each accompanied with the kindest expressions of fraternal sympathy and brotherly love.

On the 14th of October, the Relief Committee was relieved by the organization of the

MASONIC BOARD OF RELIEF,

with the following officers:

M. W. DeWitt C. Cregier, 271, Grand Master, President,
R. W. H. F. Holcomb. 141, D. D. G. M., Vice President,
R. E. Wiley M. Egan, 211, Grand Commander K. T., Treasurer,
W. Geo. K. Hazlitt, 211, Recording Secretary,
Ed. J. Hill, 211, Corresponding Secretary.

AND MEMBERS.

W. Geo. R. McClellan, 141,   W. Walter A. Stevens, 393,
W. D. J. Avery, 411,   W. G. C. Smith, 209,
W. T. T. Gurney, 211,   W. C. J. Franks, 410.
W. C. H. Brenan, 411.

The Master and Wardens of each Lodge in the city, were appointed a special committee, to ascertain the whereabouts, the condition and the wants of their respective members, and report the same to the proper officers of the Board, that the needy might be cared for. The officers and members of the Board were also divided into committees, to whom were assigned various duties incident to the occasion. This occupied nearly their whole time. All the Brethren constituting the Board were more or less sufferers by the fire, and a number of them found it necessary to devote some time to their own affairs, in order to provide for themselves and families. Thus, while the work of relief was increasing, the help and facilities to meet the demand became inadequate; consequently, on the 24th of October, changes and additions were made in both officers and members, and continued until the final adjournment, as follows:

   M. W. DeWitt C. Cregier, 271, President,
   R. W. H. F. Holcomb, 141, Vice President,
   R. E. W. M. Egan, 211, Treasurer,
   Harry Duvall, 271, Recording Secretary,
   Ed. J. Hill, 211, Corresponding Secretary,
   James Morison, 141, Superintendent.

MEMBERS.

W. T. T. Gurney, 211,	W. Geo. R. McClellan, 141,
W. D. J. Avery, 411,	W. C. J. Franks, 410,
W. John Feldkamp, 557,	W. J. H. Miles, 211,
W. E. Powell, M. D., 33,	W. John Sutton, 310,
W. D. H. Kilmore, 209,	W. J. E. Church, 160,
W. A. M. Thomson, 311,	I. W. Congdon, 526,
E. Ronayne, 639.	

From this date the rooms were kept open daily from 9 A. M. to 5 P. M., (Sundays excepted). For some time the meetings of the Board were held twice each week; subsequently but once; at which time matters connected with applications, and other business, was transacted.

The work in hand required careful supervision, involving much time and labor. It was therefore deemed proper that the Secretary and Superintendent should give their undivided attention to the business of the Board, granting them such additional assistance as might be required.

The Superintendent received all goods donated, and purchased such as were required; also, attending to the outside business generally.

The Recording Secretary took charge of, and issued the supplies, received all applications, and recorded the entire transactions pertaining to the Board. These two officers were each paid one hundred dollars per month. Assistants, to visit and investigate the condition and necessities of applicants, and perform other services, were paid from two to three dollars per day.

MASONIC BOARD OF RELIEF. 7

The President, Recording Secretary and Superintendant, were constituted an Executive Committee, who held daily meetings, to consider applications.

In nearly all letters acompanying the donations, the instructions as to the disposition thereof were explicit, and it may be worthy of note that these letters, coming, as they did, from so many different parts of the Continent, should contain language almost identical, viz : that the donations were intended "*for the relief of worthy Master Masons, their widows and orphans, who were sufferers by the fire of the eighth and ninth of October.*" Under these instructions, those who became the agents of the donors, resolved that the funds should be disbursed fairly, justly, and to those designated by the givers; and that all applicants therefor be properly vouched for, not only as being worthy, but as having suffered by the fire.

That a few who were neither worthy nor qualified, received a small amount of aid, is true ; but these exceptions were not due to carelessness on the part of those in charge, but from over-zealousness manifested by those who reccommended the applicant.

Most of the applications were attended to immediately by the Executive Committee. In some cases, however, where the request for aid seemed excessive, or where there was doubt as to, (so to speak,) the eligibility of the applicant, the matter was referred to the full Board, for their action.

A number of applications were received from brethren for loans of a considerable amount of money, for the purpose of establishing, and re-establishing, themselves in various branches of business, such as boarding houses, etc. The aggregate amount of money asked for these purposes would reach about *Two Hundred and Fifty Thousand Dollars.* Those charged with the disbursement of the fund, believed it was intended to relieve the *immediate* necessities of Masons and their families, caused by the fire; they therefore felt obliged, in view of the general instructions of the donors, and for other obvious reasons, to decline granting such applications.

In most cases, where artizans required tools in order to ply their vocations, and thereby provide for themselves and families, they were freely supplied. Among a large number of such applications, three only were refused, viz :—one required tools to the amount of four hundred dollars ; another asked for tools and machinery which would cost one thousand seven hundred and fifty dollars. The other application was from a brother engaged in the practice of law, who requested a law library and office furniture, estimated to cost a trifle over four hundred and fifty dollars. Other cases might be cited, to show that refusals to grant the aid asked for, were sometimes absolutely necessary, to keep within the bounds of propriety, not to say justice ; but those referred to are deemed sufficient.

As a matter of prudence, it was deemed best to procure whatever was required by applicants, instead of giving money, because we were then enabled to purchase in quantities, and avail ourselves of the liberal advantages offered by our merchants and dealers generally. In some cases contracts were made for supplies; this proved to the benefit of all concerned.

Where brethren desired to go to other cities to seek employment, transportation was immediately secured, and a small amount of cash in addition was given for other expenses.

During several months succeeding the fire, many brethren reached Chicago from abroad, and upon their arrival found themselves in straightened circumstances; in some cases with families dependent upon them. Our Lodges were utterly unable to respond to their call for aid, and as these brethren were in no way sufferers by the fire, the board felt a delicacy in using any of the fund in hand, for their relief. Nevertheless, the needy ones were Masons, and under ordinary circumstances they would have found succor. But this, at the time, was quite out of the question. It was therefore resolved by the Board, that all cases of this kind be referred to the Grand Master, who was empowered to render such assistance from the fund as he might deem proper. Pursuant to these instructions, a number of brethren from various jurisdictions have been assisted, and we believe, with few exceptions, they were in every way worthy, as the records will show. We mention one case of interest, viz : a brother—a clergyman—on his way to California with an invalid daughter, while en route to this city, was robbed of his money. Arriving in Chicago, he found himself destitute, and making himself known, requested two second class tickets to San Francisco, which were furnished him by order of the Grand Master. Through the fraternal kindness of Bro. E. St. John, of the C., R. I. & P. R. R. Co., the brother was furnished with letters which secured to him and his daughter the privileges of first class fare over all the roads to their destination. The brother reached his home in safety, and soon after sent a letter expressing his grateful acknowledgments for the favor and inclosing a check for the full amount advanced to him.

The courtesy of the Railroad Companies in this case, as well as many others of similar character, render the Board sensible of their obligations to the officers of the several Railroad Companies represented in our city, for the liberal concessions made in matters of transportation, and for which we desire to express our grateful acknowledgments.

For a time, subsequent to the fire, many brethren came to Chicago expecting to realize large wages for their services, and when they found they could secure but a trifle more than they had been accustomed to receive, sorely disappointed and anxious to return to their homes, they found themselves without the necessary means; they accordingly applied to the Board for assistance. At this time we could procure work for them at fair wages, and those who refused to avail themselves of a chance to work were allowed to depart in peace, as we did not feel at liberty, under the circumstances, to render them pecuniary aid.

Another class of applicants were Mason's relatives, mostly females, and not sufferers by the fire; but being in want, they were assisted, and the aid rendered is charged under the head of "charity." Indeed, all worthy applicants in need were freely assisted, and as a rule the aid rendered was gratefully received. Many families were provided for from the fund, during the entire winter and spring, or until they were enabled to help themselves.

But very little imposition has been practiced upon the Board, as those attempting it were promptly thwarted in their designs and called to an account for their conduct.

On the 1st of February a special report was issued, showing the transactions of the Board up to that date, and the same was sent to every Lodge who had contributed. It was also published in the daily press and Masonic Journals. This report stated that it was believed the amount of money already received would be sufficient to meet all legitimate demands. However, a considerable amount was subsequently donated. The special report will be found on page thirty.

The Board continued to hold regular sessions until the 15th of May, at which time it was resolved that no further supplies be distributed, except to widows and children, and brethren who were sick.

Applications were becoming greatly diminished, and soon after it was determined to close all accounts. The duty of caring for those in need was transferred to the several Lodges, and the expense necessary to carrying on the work of the Board was thus obviated. It was further the intention to award to each Lodge a certain amount of the surplus funds in order that they might be able to meet the demands for assistance made upon them.

On St. John's day, (June 24th,) the final meeting of the Board was held, and the President submitted the following

REPORT:

To the Officers and Members of the Masonic Board of Relief:

BRETHREN:—We are convened for the purpose of hearing the final report upon matters which have engaged your attention for the past eight months.

The continued call upon the fund sent here to assist our unfortunate brethren, has rendered it difficult to close the several accounts, and now that the report is ready, I need hardly say it has been a task occupying more time than was anticipated. However the minute and systematic manner in which the detail has been arranged, will, it is hoped, repay for the time spent, and prove satisfactory to all concerned.

As President, I shall report what perhaps concerns you most, viz :—the total receipts and expenditures of cash; and the proposed disposition of the surplus, leaving other interesting details to be laid before you by our Secretary. I may add, that the correctness of every transaction, whether it be of cash, supplies, or whatsoever, is shown by proper vouchers and other reliable evidences, which will be published for the perusal of all.

The cash, (exclusive of goods and other supplies,) received to date, from all sources, including premium on gold, is - - - - - - - $82,206.17
Add premium on $280 gold drafts subsequently rec'd   38.75
Add interest accruing on deposits in Metropolitan National Bank, New York, - - - -   844.14

Making total cash receipts, - - - $83,089.06

and has been donated from the following jurisdictions. See recapitulation of receipts, on page ninety-two.

The entire amount has been deposited with our Treasurer, as shown by his receipts.

Two additional donations, one of fifty dollars from Warren Lodge, Massachusetts, and one of twenty-seven dollars and twenty cents from Fidelity Lodge, Illinois, have come to hand since the close of cash account. These will be returned to the donors without being entered in accounts; for to retain them would change all our calculations, as will be seen presently. Of course, for these and all other amounts returned, receipts will be taken and filed among the papers.

There has been disbursed, thirty thousand six hundred and thirty-one dollars and thirty-seven cents, for the relief of three thousand one hundred and forty-five needy brethren, widows and children; most of which you have heretofore authorized at the different sessions held during our organization; to whom and for what, the Secretary's books will show. See tabular statement of distributions, page one hundred and eleven.

You know with what care and attention we have endeavored to disburse this sacred fund ; and it must be a source of great satisfaction to know that our efforts have been successful, for even amid the perplexities attending the first hours of our organization, there has been but very little imposition practiced upon this Board. No worthy brother Mason has applied for assistance and been neglected, no worthy widow or orphan has been denied assistance, nor have those who have been deemed unworthy received assistance, if we knew it.

Many of the Lodges in our State, and a few in other States, have sent us two, three, and even four separate contributions. Doubtless these noble Lodges have been actuated by an exuberance of charity which "suffereth long," etc., for it may be seen by their correspondence that many of them have been rather more generous to us than just to themselves.

Quite a number of the letters accompanying the donations state that they have drained their treasury and left themselves in debt. Indeed, I know of several Lodges who have embarrassed themselves in this particular. This evidence of their brotherly love for us should be, as I know it is, justly appreciated by the Masons of Chicago. To the end that we may practically manifest our appreciation of their kindness, and in order to avoid anything like partiality, I propose to return to all those Lodges which have sent two or more contributions, one half of the amount, with a proper explanation of our motives in so doing. The aggregate amount being two thousand two hundred and five dollars and eighty-nine cents, to lodges as follows:

LODGE.	NO.	LOCATION.	Separate Donations	Amount Received.	Amount Returned.
Solomons	196	New York	85 00		
do.	196	do.	50 00		
do.	196	do.	5 00	140 00	70 00
Greenwood	569	do.	100 00		
do.	569	do.	6 00	106 00	53 00
Gloversville	429	do.	300 00		
do.	429	do.	153 00	453 00	226 50
United Brethren		Massachusetts	110 00		
do.		do.	5 00	115 00	57 50
Plymouth		do.	200 00		
do.		do.	15 00		
do.		do.	3 28	218 28	109 14
Madison	93	New Jersey	216 00		
do.	93	do.	20 00	236 00	118 00
La Fayette	100	Connecticut	100 00		
do.	100	do.	262 00	362 00	181 00
Hartford	88	do.	100 00		
do.	88	do.	262 00	362 00	181 00
St. John's	4	do.	100 00		
do.	4	do.	262 00	362 00	181 00
Friendship	7	Illinois	100 00		
do.	7	do.	28 00	128 00	64 00
Stratton	408	do.	25 00		
do.	408	do.	25 00	50 00	25 00
Odell	401	do	53 00		
do.	401	do.	17 00	70 00	35 00
Chesterfield	445	do.	25 00		
do.	445	do.	35 00	60 00	30 00
Chatsworth	539	do.	108 25		
do.	539	do.	50 00	158 25	79 13
Jerseyville	394	do.	25 00		
do.	394	do.	45 50	70 50	35 25
Doric	319	do.	100 00		
do.	319	do.	79 00	179 00	89 50
Virden	161	do.	100 00		
do.	161	do.	20 00	120 00	60 00
Old Time	629	do.	25 00		
do.	629	do.	25 00	50 00	25 00
Toulon	93	do.	20 00		
do.	93	do.	10 00	30 00	15 00
Trio	57	do.	50 00		
do.	57	do.	100 00	150 00	75 00
Perry	95	do.	20 00		
do.	95	do.	50 00	70 00	35 00
Tolono	391	do.	15 50		
do.	391	do.	40 00	55 50	27 75
Louisville	96	do.	40 00		
do.	96	do.	37 75	77 75	38 87
Bunker Hill	151	do.	25 00		
do.	151	do.	50 00	75 00	37 50
Dallas City	235	do.	25 00		
do.	235	do.	25 00		
do.	235	do.	25 00		
do.	235	do.	25 00	100 00	50 00
Kankakee	389	do.	50 00		
do	389	do.	108 50	158 50	79 25
				$4,411 78	$2,205 89

As you have already expressed yourselves favorably upon the propriety of this proceeding, I have no doubt you will now confirm it.

In addition to the foregoing amount, thirty dollars, donated by Wyoming Chapter, order of Eastern Star, Illinois, will be returned, as we are informed by letter it was money collected for paraphrenalia incident to that society, and could not easily be spared.

Particular attention has invariably been given to the instructions in letters accompanying donations, and when there was any doubt inquiry was made to the proper parties for information. In a number of cases, money was donated from Chapters, for the relief of "*Companions;*" in others, from Commanderies, for the benefit of "*Sir Knights.*"

Our mission was to aid *Master Masons*, and as there were two Committees of well known brethren, organized for the special purpose of attending to R. A. Masons and Knights Templar, we have paid over to said Committees all money that was clearly intended for the brethren named, amounting to nine hundred and forty-eight dollars and fifty cents, received from the following bodies:

Clinton Commandery K. T., Mt. Vernon, Ohio,				$50 00
St. John's	do.	do. Youngstown, Ohio,		37 50
Youngstown, R. A. C. No. 93,		do. do.		
Clinton	do.	No. 26, Mt. Vernon, Ohio,		50 00
Mt. Pulaski	do.	No. 121, Mt. Pulaski, Ill.,		50 00
Edgar	do.	No. 32, Paris, Ill.,		50 00
Havana	do.	No. 86, Havana, Ill.,		75 00
Kedron	do.	No. 138, Mt. Auburn, Ill.,		25 00
Markwell	do.	No. 30, Lansing, Iowa,		10 00
Lincoln	do.	No. 53, Crown Point, Ind.,		25 00
St. John's	do.	No. 57, Fort Monroe, Va.,		40 00
Newport	do.	No. Newport, R. I.,		100 00
Union	do.	No. 7, New Jersey,		100 00
Allen	do.	No. 203, Allentown, Pa.,		25 00
Columbia	do.	No. 91, Philadelphia, Pa.,		100 00
Gate of Temple	do.	No. 208, Brooklyn, N. Y.,		50 00
Adams	do.	No. 205, Adams, N. Y.,		50 00
Idaho	do.	No. Idaho City, (gold)		100 00
Add premium on gold draft				11 00
				$948 50

It is proper to state, that a considerable amount sent by R. A. Chapters was expressly designated for the aid of Master Masons; such therefore was retained.

The Craft of Maryland, through their Grand Master, sent a draft for two thousand three hundred and four dollars and sixty-two cents, and the letter accompanying it instructed that the amount should be distributed "among the sufferers *generally*." In answer to a letter of inquiry as to whether the word "generally" was intended to include others than Masons, the Grand Master of Maryland replied, that it was so intended. Upon my suggestion that the Chicago Relief and Aid Society was better prepared to reach the sufferers *generally*, than this Board, the Grand Master of Maryland concurred, and instructed that the amount be handed to that body, which was accordingly done, and the receipt therefor is on file. See contributions from Maryland, on page sixty-five.

Brethren, I now come to a subject upon which much has been said by a few, and upon which I have bestowed considerable time and thought. It is the aid to be rendered our Lodges as such, not only those who were burned out, but also those who escaped that misfortune.

It will be found that the members of some of our Lodges have been assisted to a far greater extent than those of other Lodges. That is, there has been a great nominal disproportion in this particular, if we take their respective memberships as a basis.

I have revolved this matter in my mind, in order to arrive at a just conclusion, and the result reached is, that however much or however little each Lodge has received, it should be regarded as an index of their respective wants; because we assume that our brethren applied for and received what their necessities required. Hence, this became a part of the legitimate disbursement, and should cut no figure in their proportion of the surplus. I am persuaded that that this view is just and proper, and upon due consideration I think you will concur in it. Nevertheless, we shall show just what the members of each Lodge have received of the fund, in supplies, etc.

There is another important fact which has a great bearing in this connection; it is, that many of our Lodges have but a very limited membership, and are not, therefore, as able to withstand their misfortunes as those Lodges that have a much larger number upon their rolls. For instance, we have thirty-one chartered Lodges, ranging in membership from two hundred and ninety-three to eighteen, each being a lodge of itself; the smaller one is subject to nearly the same expenses as those with larger membership, and yet, one has but a few to bear the burdens, while the other has many. I allude to this not as the real basis of our proposal, but simply to show that it has not been lost sight of. Hence, we conclude that the larger the Lodge the smaller the *per capita*, and the smaller the Lodge the larger the *per capita*.

During the great fire, eighteen Lodges were burned out, with losses of more or less magnitude, but I know of no way to meet the question upon the basis of loss. Even the Lodges that were not burned out have members who greatly suffered by the fire, consequently they, like their more unfortunate sisters, have nominal or indirect claims to our consideration; of these there are thirteen. Lodges, U. D., we have not considered, for several reasons; the principal one being, that their members in the main are in fact members of other city Lodges and have therefore been duly considered.

To the eighteen Lodges burned out, we have set apart the sum of twenty thousand two hundred and sixty-seven dollars, being an average of eleven hundred and twenty-five dollars and ninety-four cents to each Lodge. Taking the resident membership of each Lodge at the time of the fire, from our Grand Lodge records, (of course non-residents cannot properly be counted in this case,) we have graded the Lodges, and awarded an amount in proportion to their respective membership, and I submit the following as the result.

NOTE.—The Lodges named on the following page received the amounts allotted to them, except South Park Lodge, No. 662, which declined to accept the trust.

BURNED OUT LODGES.

GRADUATION.	Name of Lodge.	No.	No. of Mem.	Amount per Member.	Total.
Lodges f'm 250 to 300 memb's	Oriental	33	293	@ $ 6.00	$1,758 00
" " 200 to 250 "	Kilwinning	311	220	" 7.00	1,540 00
	Wm. B. Warren	209	176	" 8.00	1,408 00
	Garden City	141	171	" 8.00	1,368 00
	Germania	182	165	" 8.00	1,320 00
	Dearborn	310	161	" 8.00	1,288 00
" " 125 to 200 "	Waubansia	160	160	" 8.00	1,280 00
	Blair	393	160	" 8.00	1,280 00
	Blaney	271	152	" 8.00	1,216 00
	Covenant	526	146	" 8.00	1,168 00
	Chicago	437	124	" 9.00	1,116 00
" " 100 to 125 "	Ashlar	308	108	" 9.00	972 00
	H. W. Bigelow	438	108	" 9.00	972 00
	Thos. J. Turner	409	88	" 10.00	880 00
" " 75 to 100 "	Mithra	410	78	" 10.00	780 00
	Accordia	277	76	" 10.00	760 00
" " 50 to 75 "	Lincoln Park	611	63	" 11.00	693 00
" " 25 to 50 "	Keystone	639	39	" 12.00	468 00
					20,267 00

Average per Lodge,--$1,125 94

To the non-burned out Lodges, under the views heretofore expressed, we have awarded just one-half the *per capita* to those Lodges having same grade or membership as determined for burned out Lodges, which amounts to Five Thousand Three Hundred and One Dollars, or an average of Four Hundred and Seven Dollars and Seventy-seven cents to each, as follows:

LODGES NOT BURNED OUT.

GRADUATION.	Name of Lodge.	No.	No. of Mem.	Amount per Member.	Total.
Lodges f'm 250 to 300 memb's	Cleveland	211	318	@ $ 3.00	$ 954 00
	Home	508	156	" 4.00	624 00
" " 125 to 200 "	Hesperia	411	134	" 4.00	536 00
	Pleiades	478	134	" 4.00	536 00
" " 100 to 125 "	Union Park	610	100	" 4.50	450 00
" " 75 to 100 "	National	596	83	" 5.00	415 00
	Apollo	642	76	" 5.00	380 00
" " 50 to 75 "	D. C. Cregier	643	69	" 5.50	379 50
	Lessing	557	61	" 5.50	335 50
" " 25 to 50 "	Landmark	422	46	" 6.00	276 00
	South Park	662	26	" 6.00	156 00
Less than 25	Herder	669	19	" 7.00	133 00
	Waldeck	674	18	" 7.00	126 00
					$5,301 00

Average per Lodge,--$ 407 77

I suggest that these awards be made upon the express condition, that each Lodge receiving the amount, shall amend their By-Laws, establishing a charity fund, of which the several amounts here named shall constitute the nucleus. This fund may be used for any purpose, still, if used for current expenses, the amount so used will be due to said charity fund.

This will be observing the intentions of the donors, and we can then say, thanks to our Brethren from abroad, that every Lodge in Chicago has a charity fund, separate and distinct from its general fund. I think it will be conceeded by every mason in our midst, that the craft of Chicago should see to it, that our brethren from abroad who may reach this city, and find themselves in distress, should be treated with that fraternal consideration which our Fellows throughout the country have extended to us. To do this under our present straightened circumstances, would be like unto the "blind leading the blind." But the Masons of Chicago are *citizens* of Chicago, and we may therefore safely predict that our present masonic misfortunes will soon be overcome, by that true courage and unexampled energy, which will soon rebuild and re-establish upon yonder black and desolate area, a great and enduring city, in which we hope, in due time, to re-construct our Temples, and extend to every true craftsman a just measure of masonic hospitality.

For a number of years we had a permanent Board of Relief in our city, which did a noble work, and exemplified the true principles of masonry. But I regret to say that this useful organization, after a time, was but poorly supported, and at length was suffered, through neglect, to die.

Brethren, I hold this to be a crying shame, a stigma upon the 4,000 masons of our city. The importance of such an organization cannot be over estimated. . What is everybody's business in general, is no one's business in particular, and for each Lodge to dispense alms is, in a measure, impracticable and liable to great abuse and imposition, while a Board of Relief would do this duty more efficiently, and with greater convenience and protection against imposters.

Such a Board should be established, to be composed of a representative from each Lodge in our city, from whom the officers would be chosen. Their duty would be to care for the needs of those *only* who come from abroad, and not for resident masons.

I assume that our Lodges will have recovered from their misfortunes in three years, and will then be in full tide of prosperity. We have, therefore, thought proper to set apart sixthousand dollars for such a Board, this to be augmented by such sums as may accrue from interest on deposit, say $600.00, (this amount is increased to $844.14, see page 23), and from sale of stock on hand, and other driblets which, when expenses to be incurred hereafter are paid, would amount to say $6,500, or about $2,200 per annum for three years. This amount being hardly adequate for the purpose, I would, as Grand Master, earnestly call upon the several Lodges in the city to contribute 25 cents per member, per annum, which would make about $1,000, or less than five per cent. interest on the funds donated to the Lodges. This with the small interest that would accrue on the unexpended portion in the hands of such Board, would give about $2,600 per year, for the next three years, for the relief of those whose needs require it. Thus, if each Lodge has a charity fund, one half the interest of which will pay their quota, the work is done.

Here we have an opportunity to resuscitate a most excellent organization upon a permanent and encouraging basis.

I earnestly pray that you will respond to it, by sending a representative, with the proposed dues, and be ready to "do unto others as they have done unto you."

Thus, my brethren, we have given an outline of our labors during the past eight months; having administered to the wants of several thousand needy applicants, and in the discharge of our delicate duties, we have, as the agents of our kind donors, endeavored to be just, as well as generous.

We have fed the hungry, clothed the naked, been instrumental in healing the sick, buried the dead, sent the weary traveler on his way rejoicing, given substantial aid to each and every Lodge in our city, and provided for the establishment of a permanent relief fund.

With this, we believe, our organization has fulfilled its mission, and it is hoped that the work has been done in accordance with the written instructions of those whose bounty we have disbursed, and that the course we have pursued will meet their approval.

But notwithstanding, we find in our hands a surplus of Twenty Thousand Dollars, which, under the circumstances, we naturally conceive belongs to those who sent it, or rather, to those whom they represent. It is not difficult, therefore, to determine how it shall be disposed of; because we think it should be clearly understood that no part of this money was sent here for the purpose of making worthless insurance good, nor to start persons in business, nor to disburse it simply because it was sent here, nor to divide among those who have no other claim except that, they want their "*share ;*" for, as before stated, these demands alone would have absorbed over three times the amount received. But we hold the object of the fund was to temporarily relieve the immediate wants of sufferers by the great fire; this accomplished, the balance should be returned. I have therefore, provided as follows :

Of the total amount sent from all quarters, we have ascertained the proportion contributed by each Grand Jurisdiction.

To all States that have sent Four Hundred Dollars and over, we propose to return their respective proportions of the whole sum received. Those which sent less than $400 is retained, since the proportion accruing therefrom would be too insignificant to return. Hence, we find these sums to be 2.05-100 per cent. of the $20,000, while those of $400 and upwards, amount to 97.95-100 per cent. The former sum, like all driblets, will be placed in the permanent relief fund.

Individual Lodges which have contributed $400 and upward have been considered upon the same basis independently, the amounts due them being deducted from that due their Grand Lodge.

In a number of cases, money amounting to several hundred dollars, was sent from the "craft," and not from any particular Lodge. All such sums are credited to the *Jurisdiction* from whence it came.

It would be entirely impracticable to return this surplus to each particular Lodge. Indeed, in the majority of cases it would not amount to enough to pay for the trouble. But we find that by aggregating these small amounts, in many cases it makes a handsome sum.

To the State of New York we return their proportion for the benefit of the "Hall and Asylum Fund;" one of the grandest Masonic benevolent institutions ever projected by the fraternity. In all other cases it is returned to the "Charity Fund" of the Grand Lodge, with suitable explanations, and giving a list of their respective subordinates which have contributed the amounts. Thus it will be known to whom the several Grand Lodges are indebted for the donation.

I feel confident that the individual Lodges of our sister Jurisdictions will fully appreciate this disposition of the surplus, and will commend your thoughtful interest in their behalf. Indeed, I have already received letters from Grand Officers of several Jurisdictions, to whom I had intimated your intentions, and they have expressed themselves pleased with the idea.

The following tabulated statement will show the manner of disposing of the surplus:

TABULAR STATEMENT OF SURPLUS RETURNED.

JURISDICTION.	Total amount Received.	Amount Returned to Lodges that sent more than one donation	Balance after deducting the amount returned to Lodges that sent more than one Donation	Per cent. of Surplus.	Proportion to be Returned each Jurisdiction.	Amt. Returned to Lodges that sent over $400.	Amount Returned to the Grand Lodge of each Jurisdiction.	Total amount Returned each Jurisdiction.
Maine	$450 00	$	$450 00	0.56	$112 00	$	$112 00	$112 00
New Hampshire	200 00		200 00					
Massachusetts	7,402 71	166 64	7,236 07	9.04	1,808 00	124 93	1,683 07	1,974 64
Rhode Island	100 00		100 00					
Connecticut	1,872 18		1,329 18	1.66	332 00		332 00	875 00
New York	18,388 85	543 00	18,039 35	22.55	4,510 00	1,105 83	3,404 17	4,859 50
New Jersey	4,441 20	349 50	4,323 20	5.40	1,080 00		1,080 00	1,198 00
Pennsylvania	9,607 15	118 00	9,607 15	12.00	2,400 00	249 60	2,150 40	2,400 00
Maryland	50 50		50 50					
Virginia	117 00		117 00					
District of Columbia	3,022 30		3,022 30	3.78	756 00		756 00	756 00
South Carolina	25 00		25 00					
Louisiana	400 00		400 00	0.50	100 00		100 00	100 00
Ohio	699 00		699 00	0.87	174 00		174 00	174 00
Indiana	1,069 00		1,069 00	1.33	266 00		266 00	266 00
Illinois	12,917 75	801 25	12,116 50	15.14	3,028 00		3,028 00	3,829 25
Kentucky	1,988 75		1,988 75	2.48	496 00		496 00	496 00
Minnesota	75 00		75 00					
Iowa, (Lodges,)	818 25		818 25	1.02	204 00		204 00	204 00
Iowa, (Chapters,)	881 25		881 25	1.10	220 00		220 00	220 00

MASONIC BOARD OF RELIEF.   23

Missouri	1,450 00		1,450 00	1.81	362 00	362 00
Kansas	759 50		759 50	0.95	190 00	190 00
Nebraska	680 90	227 50	453 40	0.57	114 00	114 00
Nevada	555 00		555 00	0.69	138 00	138 00
California	7,501 78		7,501 78	9.37	1,874 00	1,874 00
Oregon	100 00		100 00			
Idaho	111 00		111 00			
Colorado	42 00		42 00			
Dakota	60 50		60 50			
Utah	230 00		230 00			
Canada	3,978 47		3,978 47	4.97	994 00	994 00
Quebec	644 00		644 00	0.85	170 00	170 00
New Foundland	461 00		461 00	0.58	116 00	116 00
Panama	584 85		584 85	0.73	146 00	146 00
New Mexico	100 00		100 00			
British India	26 65					
England	394 63		394 63			
	$82,206 17	$2,205 89	$80,000 28	97.95	$19,590 00	$1,480 36	$18,109 64	$21,795 89

NOTE.—Interest on deposits, $844.14, and premium on gold drafts, $38.75, amounting to $882.89, have been received since the foregoing table was made, and, therefore, not included.

The amount set apart to be returned, not including the amounts returned to Lodges that sent more than one donation, was $20,000. The amount actually returned was $19,590, or 97.95-100 per cent. of $20,000. The balance, $410, or 2.05-100 per cent., is accounted for by the fact that no returns were made to Jurisdictions that sent less than $400.

Memorandum of Lodges that donated over $400, to whom returns were made, and the amount deducted from the proportion due their Jurisdiction.

First, the name of the Lodge is given, next the amount donated, then the proportion the amount sent bears to the total amount received from the State; and, lastly, the amount returned to the Lodge:

NEW YORK.

Lodge	Donated	Per cent.	Returned
Independent Royal Arch Lodge, No. 2,	$500 00	2.77 per cent.	$124 92
Masters Lodge, No. 5,	500 00	2.77 "	124 92
Holland Lodge, No. 8,	1,070 00	5.93 "	267 44
Montauk Lodge, No. 286,	500 00	2.77 "	124 92
Rising Star Lodge, No. 450,	650 00	3.60 "	162 36
Merchants Lodge, No. 702,	1,205 00	6.68 "	301 27
			$1,105 83

MASSACHUSETTS.

Lodge	Donated	Per cent.	Returned
Jos. Warren Lodge	$ 500 00	6.91 per cent.	$124 93

PENNSYLVANIA.

Lodge	Donated	Per cent.	Returned
St. John's Lodge, No. 219,	$ 500 00	5.20 per cent.	$124 80
Shekinah Lodge, No. 246,	500 00	5.20 "	124 80
			$249 60

Our work has been of the most delicate character, but I can truly say that this Board, and its agents, have endeavored to disburse the fund with discretion, and with an eye single to the welfare of all concerned. Notwithstanding this, it would be unreasonable to expect that these efforts have been entirely satisfactory to all; and if there are any who think they have cause to complain, let them put themselves in your place, and ask the question, in all seriousness, if they would have done better for the sufferers, better for the donors, and better for the good name of Masonry in Chicago. Let it not be forgotten, also, that a number of the members of this Board were, by the calamity that created this organization, reduced to comparative beggary, but they forgot themselves and went to work with a will, to aid others no worse off.

I have seen members of this Board, presenting a worthy example, standing here day after day, at work, without the hope of reward, needing for themselves just such assistance as they were rendering to others, but declining to accept anything. Yea, it is an honorable and praiseworthy record, that although nearly every member of this Board were great sufferers by the fire, yet the record will show, that with few exceptions, they have received absolutely nothing from the fund, because of their peculiar relations with it.

The large amount of money that has been sent me has been paid over to our Treasurer. Every Lodge, or individual, who has contributed, is recorded; and we propose to publish this in full, and send to every Lodge, and other donor, to the end that if any have sent money not so recorded, they may have a chance to let it be known. Indeed, we now and hereafter, invite the closest scrutiny into all our affairs, and if any one shall detect error, or even ambiguity, in our records, we earnestly request that attention may be called to it, to the end that explanation may be made known; and that our labors may be thoroughly examined into, I earnestly recommend that the M. W. Grand Masters of three of our sister Jurisdictions be requested to make us a visit, to examine, investigate and report upon the justice and propriety of our transactions. The high character of such distinguished Masons is sufficient to justify you in endorsing this suggestion. Should these brethern respond to our invitation, we cannot promise them such a reception as we would like, yet we will endeavor to bestow such attention as may be in our power, and will, of course, assume the expense incident to their visit. When such Committee shall pass upon our proceedings, I would recommend that a sufficient number of the general report be suitably printed, and a copy forwarded to every donor.

Our Secretary and Superintendent have given their whole time to this work, and have performed their duties in a satisfactory manner. Upon the former the bulk of the work has been imposed. I would, therefore, recommend that $200 be paid Bro. Duvall, as extra remuneration. To Bro. Morrison, our Superintendent, the sum of $100. I also recommend that the stock now on hand be disposed of as you may deem proper.

In conclusion, brethren, permit me, in behalf of the fraternity, to thank you, individually and collectively, for your zealous and voluntary labors in the holy cause of charity and brotherly love. May you never be called upon to do duty on account of such a fearful disaster as that of the ever memorable 8th and 9th of October last. And for your forbearance, co-operation and fraternal respect, I beg to return my thanks.

For my part in this great work I have but little to say, except this: that nothing but my official position, would have induced me to assume the delicate responsibilities incident to the extraordinary occasion; but my duty was plain, I therefore had no disposition to evade it. I have endeavored to discharge the trust imposed upon me by my position, with integrity, justice and candor. The result is before you, and will be before the Masonic world.

Dewitt C. Cregier,
President.

The foregoing report was received, and, on motion, all the recommendations and suggestions therein contained were adopted, with one dissenting vote. The Secretary's report and accounts were also unanimously approved.

The President was, by vote of the Board, requested, with such assistance as might be required, to prepare and have printed, a general report of the transactions. Also, to dispose of the stock on hand. Whereupon, the "Board of Masonic Relief" adjourned *sine die*.

These instructions were carried out as soon as practicable; the goods and supplies in store were placed in the hands of William A. Butters & Co., Auctioneers, and sold.

CHICAGO, Aug. 2nd, 1872.

MR. DEWITT C. CREGIER, City :—Dear Sir :—We hand you check for Five Hundred and Sixteen 53-100 ($516.53) Dollars, being amount realized from sale, for account of the Masonic Board of Relief.

WM. A. BUTTERS & CO., Auctioneers.

The loss incurred upon sale of the goods was, by order of the Board, charged to charity account.

The names of all applicants are on record, but for obvious reasons have been omitted in this report.

The following Circular and papers, were sent to each Lodge in the city :

CHICAGO, June 26th, 1872.

To the W. M., Wardens and Brethren of   Lodge No   ,
A. F. and A. Masons :

DEAR BRETHREN :—The Board of Masonic Relief organized in October last, for the purpose of distributing the funds and other aid sent here for the relief of needy Masons and their families, who were sufferers by the great fire, deeming it expedient to bring its labors to a close, held a final meeting on the 24th instant, at which time it was decided to transfer to the several Lodges in the city, the duty of providing aid for their respective members and others having claims upon them, who may now or hereafter require assistance, and in order to carry out this object, it was deemed proper to apportion to the Lodges in the city an amount in cash from the surplus on hand, in proportion to their respective resident memberships, as shown by the Grand Lodge records.

The membership of your Lodge, in Oct. last, was   . Your apportionment, as decided by the Board of Relief, is $ *per capita*, making a total of $. In addition to this it appears from the records of the Board of Relief, that individual members of your Lodge have received, in the aggregate, assistance from the common fund, to the amount of $, which, with the amount in cash, as herein proposed, makes a grand total of $ disbursed from the relief fund for the benefit of   Lodge No.

The amount of cash apportioned to the several Lodges, is awarded upon the express condition, that each of said Lodges will accept the same as a "CHARITY FUND," to be held separate and distinct from its general fund, and be accounted for as such upon your books and records. And that you will amend your By-Laws in such manner as may be necessary to fully provide therefor. It being understood that these conditions shall in no wise interfere with the use or expenditure of this fund for any legitimate purpose which the Lodge may lawfully determine. The object being that when said fund is used for other than purely charity purposes, said fund may be credited with the amount and be repaid the same when practicable, and should be with interest. This provision, however, will be determined by each Lodge.

Furthermore, the Board of Relief, at the meeting aforesaid, having provided a liberal sum of money towards the establishment in our city of a permanent Board of Relief, in the organization and success of which every Lodge should take a deep interest, and have a voice, we, as Grand Master, do most earnestly and fraternally urge upon every Lodge in our city to send one member thereof as a representative, the whole number to constitute said proposed Board, who will, when organized, by selecting proper officers, become the custodians and almoners of said fund, together with that which may hereafter be subscribed thereto, and after such organization shall be effected, we do hereby, in behalf of the craft of Chicago, and in the name of that greatest of all virtues, "*Blessed Charity*," pray, that each Lodge will, for the present, come forward and assist in maintaining this proposed and much needed and hitherto neglected Masonic Organization. This, we think, can be done under present circumstances, if each Lodge will contribute, say twenty-five cents per member, per annum, which would be less than five per cent. interest on the amount awarded to the Lodges as a Charity Fund.

By this means the craft of Chicago may in some small measure reciprocate the good deeds of our Brethren everywhere. Let us provide for the needs of those of our worthy Brethren who may come among us from abroad and find themselves in distress, for it should be for those only that this fund is created, and not for resident Brethren.

The practice of Charity is a duty and a pleasure, which we, as Masons and Christians, should seek to discharge, in the most efficient manner. In no way can it be so effectively and conveniently done as through an organization such as is herein referred to.

We trust the Lodges will take action upon this important question at the earliest practicable time.

In behalf of the late Board of Relief, I am Fraternally,

David C. Cregier
      Late President.

The following is suggested as a By-Law, to create and maintain a Charity Fund:

I. This Lodge shall have a "CHARITY FUND," which shall include all moneys that may be donated, or in any other way designed therefor. Both principal and interest of which, when *permanently* disbursed, shall be for charitable purposes, and not otherwise.

II. Provided, however, that the Lodge, or its duly authorized Officers, (here name such officers, whether trustees or others,) may at any time, when deemed necessary, *temporarily* transfer the whole, or any amount of said "charity fund" to the general treasury, the same to be refunded, with interest at   per cent.

III. No portion of the "charity fund" shall be permanently expended, except by consent of three-fourths of the members present at a stated communication of the Lodge.

         CHICAGO, June 26th, 1872.

TO WHOM IT MAY CONCERN:

Lodges desiring to amend their By-Laws, to meet the above requirements, without regard to time, are hereby empowered so to do, and this shall be sufficient authority therefor. Make due return to me of your doings by virtue hereof.

Given under my hand and seal, this 26th day of June, 5872.

[SEAL.] *Deurd C Augier*
            Grand Master.

To Whom It May Concern:

This is to certify, that we, the W. M., Wardens and Brethren of   Lodge No.   A. F. and A. M., in Lodge assembled, do hereby accept the sum of $, awarded us from the surplus in the hands of the late Board of Masonic Relief, and do hereby, in consideration thereof, agree to conform to the conditions and requirements, viz: That we will amend our By-Laws, creating a Charity Fund, to the credit of which the sum herein named shall be placed.

                  W. M.
[SEAL.]   Attest, .   Sec'y.

The Lodges generally acquiesced in the requirements, and most of them have sent a representative to the permanent Board of Relief, which is now fully organized.

SPECIAL REPORT OF THE BOARD OF MASONIC RELIEF.

          Chicago, February 1st, 1872.

To the Masonic Fraternity throughout the United States, Canada and Elsewhere:

Brethren :—The calamity which laid waste and destroyed the fairest portion of our city, in October last, entailed upon all classes of our people a degree of misfortune and distress which has evoked the sympathy and condolence of the civilized world.

The Masonic Fraternity, as such, of this city, have, in common with others, experienced a sad reverse.

A number of beautiful Halls, together with the records, jewels, paraphernalia and other property of eighteen Lodges, two Chapters, one Council, two Commanderies, and four bodies of the Scottish Rite, were totally destroyed.* Thus, in a few hours, the Craft of Chicago were reduced from a condition of comparative affluence and comfort, to that of poverty and distress. For a moment the brethren of our city were enveloped in a cloud of misfortune, whose density was indeed appalling. But, happily, in every community, there were hundreds of Freemasons who soon dispelled the darkness. As *citizens* they have not only manifested a deep and heartfelt interest in the welfare of our stricken people, by generous contributions of money and supplies for the relief of our *citizens generally*, but in addition to this, the great Brotherhood, from every quarter, have sent munificent gifts of money and supplies for the relief of their needy brethren, and the widows and orphans of deceased Masons.

Brethren, the promptness with which your noble charity has been forwarded, has proved most effectual, and the kind words accompanying your acceptable gifts, will linger in the hearts of those who have felt the warm glow of fraternal charity, long after the black and hideous monuments, which are evidences of our calamity, have passed away.

Charity has ever been esteemed among Masons the crowning virtue, and its practical exemplification illustrates your devotion to the principles of our benign institution, and goes far to strengthen and embellish the character of a fraternity, who have for so many, many years, given proofs of powerful and generous qualities.

The brethren of Chicago find themselves confronted with a debt of gratitude, alike profound, formidable and sacred. It is this sacredness that induces us to state, that, although our task of caring for the needy is not by any means finished, yet we deem it not only just and proper, but a most agreeable duty to say that your unequalled benificence and liberality have placed in our hands a fund that we believe to be ample to meet the demands which can be legitimately made upon it. We, therefore, with that gratitude which words are inadequate to express, take pleasure in announcing that further contributions to our present resources will not be necessary.

FINAL REPORT OF THE

It is not our purpose at this time to render a detailed report of our agency in your behalf; this we hope to do to *every donor* as soon as practicable, but we may give a synopsis of what has been done, to date.

The Board of Relief is composed of a President, Vice-President, Treasurer, Recording and Corresponding Secretaries, Superintendent and Thirteen Members, who hold meetings once each week.

The rooms of the Board are kept open daily, (except Sunday,) from 9 A. M. until 5 P. M. The business is conducted by the Recording Secretary and Superintendent, with such assistance as is found necessary to dispense your bounty.

The Board have endeavored to devote the funds pursuant to instructions, viz: to those who are worthy and rendered needy by the great fire.

Since the organization, about three thousand persons consisting of brethren, widows and children, have been substantially aided with everything calculated to relieve their wants and enhance comfort.

A very full and minute record has been kept of all our transactions, which, in due time, will be submitted to you, giving the name of Lodge or person, and amount of each contribution received.

```
The total cash receipts, from all sources, which have been de-
    posited with the Treasurer, is............................$68,556 00
In hands of brethren at various locations, subject to order of the
    Treasurer,............................................... 9,696 43

            Total cash,......................................$78,252 43
Estimated value of supplies received,........................ 5,136 63

            Total amount of cash and supplies received,......$83,389 06
Total amount cash expenditures to date,..........$19,257 79
Estimated value of supplies distributed,.......... 4,136 63
Cash balance on hand and subject to order,........ 58,994 64
Estimated value of supplies on hand,.............. 1,000 00

                                                 $83,389 06  $83,389 06
Total amount of cash and supplies received,................$83,379 06
    "       "       "       "       distributed,.............. 23,394 42
    "       "       "       "       on hand,..................$59,994 64
Total cash contributions from different States,.............$78,252 43
```

In addition to the above, about $400.00 will accrue from premium on gold, and possibly a small amount for interest on deposits.

It will be observed that none of the Lodges, as such, have received any assistance from the above fund, although the majority of them, by reason of the total destruction of their Halls and property, including, in many cases, their accumulated funds, (making a loss in the aggregate of over $90,000.00,) together with the worthlessness of their insurance, involves much embarrassment. Nevertheless, the terrible ordeal through which the craft of Chicago have passed, has neither scorched their zeal nor abated their energy, but through your sympathy and aid, Freemasonry still survives in our city, and we trust that in the future, as in the past, brethren, from wheresoever they may hail, will find in Chicago a continuation of generous hospitality, created by warm and grateful hearts, and evinced by the strong grip of friendship and brotherly love.

Fraternally,

President.

BRETHREN :—In addition to the report of the President, and the statements and tables furnished by the Secretary, the members of the Board desire to say, in conclusion, that it seems unnecessary to prolong this record. The foregoing is ample and full. Nothing has been omitted that will prevent you from having a clear understanding of every detail connected with our transactions.

You know what we would say of your loving, fraternal generosity, if the poverty of language did not prevent. Brethren, you have fed the hungry, clothed the naked, and bound up the wounds of the afflicted. Your reward is in the Grand Lodge above. For, "Inasmuch as ye have done *it* unto one of the least of these my brethren, ye have done *it* unto me."

Thousands of truly thankful hearts are invoking the Divine blessing upon you and yours: and not until "the wicked cease from troubling, and the weary are at rest," will it ever be known how much humanity is indebted for the example of our noble Brotherhood. You have erected a monument to Masonry as enduring as time. Temples will decay; empires disappear, amid the cycles of coming ages; enemies traduce and traitors endeavor to compass its destruction; still it will stand, because our *Sovereign Grand Master* is the Master Builder, and you his faithful craftsmen.

For a short time. after the destruction of our city men stood aghast! The calamity was so appalling that men shrunk from is contemplation. Standing amid the terrible desolation, the question involuntarily sprang from the lips of thousands, "What shall we do?" Brethren, it was literally true "that there were no designs upon the trestle board, and the craft were in confusion." Were we in a time like this worthy of condemnation if, for the moment, we did forget that Masonry, as the instrument of a Beneficent Father, had, for ages, been inculcating and enforcing the practice of the Divine virtues of Brotherly Love, Relief and Truth? The losses, the trials and sufferings of our people had nearly lost us our faith; but when we turned from the dreary, chilling picture of our distress, we saw the beautiful tendrils of brotherly love clustering around a Father's promise. We then saw, with Faith's unbounded vision, that succor was at hand. We then felt the throbbings of the great fraternal heart, as they were borne to us by every breeze and from every clime.

Brethren, you inspired us with both faith and hope; strength took the place of weakness, and men grappled with the stern facts of the hour with a determination that has been unparalleled in the history of disaster. But for your love for the noble tenets of our profession; but for a world's generous response to our needs, Chicago would now be slumbering in her despair, instead of rising, Phœnix-like, from the ashes of her desolation. *When you fed and clothed us, you rebuilded our desolate places.*

In conclusion, we desire to present, for your very fraternal consideration and esteem, the President of this Board, who, by his untiring attention to his duties, has been able to present you a report which reflects so much credit upon the craft of our city and State. You cannot apprehend the perplexities which surrounded his labors. He was, *de-facto*, your almoner.

Our Treasurer, whose fidelity was never questioned before the fire, cannot, surely, be questioned now.

Our Secretary has won for himself a distinction that entitles him to your entire confidence and esteem. Neither the President, Treasurer, Secretary or Superintendent need any praise at our hands. The record, the proof of their zeal and fidelity is before you. If any brother require further evidence, we confidently and unhesitatingly refer him to the hundreds of our distressed brethren, the widow and the orphan, who to-day thank God that He called those brethren to these high and holy trusts.

REPORT OF THE
AUDITING COMMISSION.

Pursuant to the recommendation of the President, and with the concurrence of the Board, to invite a commission of Grand Masters from abroad, to examine and report upon the accounts and proceedings, in connection with the disbursement of the relief fund, invitations were extended to Hon. Samuel C. Perkins, Grand Master of Pennsylvania, Hon. Charles F. Stansbury, Grand Master of the District of Columbia, and Hon. Ozias P. Waters, Grand Master of Iowa, to visit Chicago and act as such commission.

These distinguished men and masons did us the honor to comply with the request, reaching Chicago, accompanied by Worshipful Brother Charles H. Kingston, Private Secretary to the Grand Master of Pennsylvania, on the seventeenth of September, 1872.

An occasional Grand Lodge was convened by the Grand Master of Illinois, and the Most Worshipful Brethren were received with the honors due their stations, and accorded such poor hospitality as the time and occasion afforded.

After interesting and fraternal addresses by each of the visitors and an interchange of social courtesies, the Grand Lodge was closed, and the commission, with Brother Kingston as Secretary, immediately entered upon the discharge of their duties.

Every book, paper, voucher or other evidence bearing upon the transactions of the Board, together with the correspondence in connection therewith, were placed at their disposal, and every assistance and facility rendered to insure a critical examination.

The subjoined exhaustive and able report of the commission speaks for itself, and leaves us little to say, except to express in behalf of the Fraternity of Chicago, our earnest and hearty thanks for the invaluable services rendered by these brethren, and a just appreciation of their generous sacrifice of valuable time and personal convenience, incident to a journey of hundreds of miles, and a lengthened absence from their important and pressing official duties.

MASONIC HALL, Chicago, Sept. 19, 1872.
M. W. DEWITT C. CREGIER,
        Grand Master of Masons of Illinois:

M. W. Sir and Brother :—The undersigned have the honor to enclose the Report which they have prepared, as embodying the result of their labors in the discharge of the duty to which your courtesy invited them, of examining the proceedings of the Masonic Board of Relief for sufferers by the great fire at Chicago, in October, 1871.

We should do injustice to our own feelings, were we to suffer the opportunity to pass, of expressing our personal appreciation of the motives which prompted the Board to desire an examination and review of the proceedings.

The action is alike honorable to the Board and an honor to the teachings of our ancient institution.

Nor can we close our labors without tendering to you, M. W. Sir, personally, and the brethren at Chicago, our sincere and fraternal thanks for the attention and courtesy shown us during our visit.

With sincere wishes for the prosperity of the M. W. Grand

Lodge of Illinois, and the earnest prayer that the Great Architect of the universe may preserve the Lodges throughout her jurisdiction from all calamity and peril,
We remain, most truly and fraternally,

Sam'l C. Perkins

Grand Master of Pennsylvania.

Chas. F. Stansbury

Grand Master of District of Columbia.

O. P. Waters,

Grand Master of Masons in Iowa.

Chas. H. Kingston

Secretary.

TO THE CONTRIBUTORS

OF THE

MASONIC RELIEF FUND

FOR THE

SUFFERERS BY THE CHICAGO FIRE.

CHICAGO, September, 5872.

The undersigned, having been honored by the Grand Master of Masons of Illinois, with a request to act as a Commission, to examine and report upon the accounts and proceedings of the Masonic Board of Relief, charged with administering the funds contributed by the Masonic Fraternity of this and other countries, for the benefit of the sufferers by the great Chicago Fire of 1871, have performed the duty assigned them; and it should be fully understood, at the outset, that this duty has been requested of the undersigned, through the voluntary act of the Board of Relief, prompted by a high sense of delicacy and honor, and not from any feeling or intimation, on the part of the donors, that any investigation was required.

The undersigned, met at the Masonic Temple, in Chicago, September 18th and 19th, 1872. Grand Master Samuel C. Perkins, of Pennsylvania, acting as President of the Commission, and Worshipful Brother Charles H. Kingston, of Pennsylvania, as Secretary.

They proceeded to make a careful examination of all the books, papers and vouchers of the Board of Relief, and of the system adopted by them for the custody and administration of the fund, and for the preservation of a record of their proceedings under the important trust confided to them.

All the books, papers and vouchers of the Board, and of its officers and committees, were submitted to the undersigned, together with the final report of the management of the fund, which exhibit, in detail, all the statistics necessary to show the very thorough and exact manner in which this important trust has been administered.

Keeping in view the fact that this fund was contributed specifically for the relief of master masons and their families who were sufferers by the great fire, the Board of Relief, from the outset, adopted the principle of satisfying themselves, personally, that each applicant relieved came within the provisions of the trust; was worthy, and in actual need of the aid granted. So far as practicable, the applicants were furnished with such articles of immediate necessity for their household and personal wants as their needs required, and the Board, by the liberality of the merchants with whom they dealt, and of the railroad companies over whose roads transportation of applicants relieved was needed, were enabled to obtain supplies and transportation at greatly reduced cost. Only a small amount was disbursed in direct appropriations of money. The Board did not regard the fund as intended to make good mere pecuniary losses by the fire, or in any sense an insurance fund, but as contributed for the temporary relief of the immediate and pressing necessities of direct sufferers by the fire.

Among the large number of applicants it was too much to

expect that no case of attempted fraud and imposition would occur. But a careful personal examination of the records of the Board and of their detailed action in individual cases, satisfied the undersigned that the greatest diligence had been exercised in their investigation; while at the same time no unnecessary formalities were permitted to exist to prevent relief being afforded promptly.

All money received for the fund was paid over to the Treasurer, and by him deposited to the credit of a separate account in bank, and paid out by checks upon orders drawn by the President and attested by the Secretary of the Board.

The immediate disbursements were made by the Secretary, under the supervision of the executive committee, and a full and detailed report was presented at each monthly meeting of the Board, examined and vouched for by a sub-committee, and approved by the Board. The books of the Secretary and Treasurer were examined and compared with the vouchers by the undersigned, and found to be correct, in every particular, and kept with a degree of accuracy and fullness of detail which cannot be too highly commended.

It was the earnestly expressed wish of all the officers and members of the Board, with the majority of whom we had the pleasure of meeting, that the undersigned would make their investigation and review thorough and searching, to the last detail, and such has been our endeavor; and this report is the result of a full and minute personal examination, influenced solely by a desire to arrive at the truth, and to declare our conclusions to the fraternity at large, as the convictions of our minds, under a due sense, as well of the obligations of the respective offices which it is our honor to hold in the craft, as of the special trust devolved upon us in this particular regard.

The entire amount of cash donations received was... $83,089 06
In addition to which supplies of goods were sent
valued at..   7,545 44
                Making a total of.................. $90,634 50
Of this amount there has been disbursed, in the relief
of applicants, allotments to Chicago Lodges, the
expenses of the Board, and a donation to Chicago
Masonic Board of Relief, as set forth, in detail, in
the report which is to be printed................$67,414 04
There has been returned to the donors a surplus of... 21,825 89
And there has been retained to meet the expenses of
printing the report, and this commission 1,394 57
                                                     ————$90,634 50

The orders drawn upon the Treasurer had not all been presented at the date of this report, nor had all the checks drawn by him been presented to the bank for payment; but the undersigned are satisfied that the money is on hand and in the bank, to the credit of his account, as Treasurer of the Board, to meet the outstanding orders and checks, on presentation.

The undersigned find that a careful, exact and clear record has been kept of every transaction, that the money received and disbursed is accurately accounted for, and that the disbursements are supported by vouchers which present, in minutest detail, the exact history of every charity bestowed, and allow every transaction to be reviewed in all its attendant circumstances. Every precaution which prudence could suggest has been taken to secure the faithful application of the fund to the beneficiaries for whom it was designed by the donors.

The detailed report prepared for publication by the Board was submitted to and carefully examined and approved by the undersigned.

It would be impossible to speak too highly of the character of the record which has been preserved of transactions so multifarious and minute, and the undersigned would do injustice to the impression made upon them by this examination should they fail to express their unqualified approbation of the manner in which the Board have administered the trust confided to them by the Fraternity.

Respectfully and Fraternally submitted by

Sam'l C. Perkins

Grand Master of Pennsylvania.

Chas. F. Stansbury

Grand Master of District of Columbia.

O. R. Waters.

Grand Master of Masons in Iowa.

Chas. H. Kingston

Secretary.

CONTRIBUTIONS

OF

MONEY AND SUPPLIES.

The following is a list of Money, Goods, Clothing, Provisions, etc., which have been received by this Board, for distribution; and also all that came before the Board was fully organized, as far as we have been able to obtain a record of the same. It is believed that we received every cent of the money forwarded to us. Previous to October 24th, quite an amount of goods had been received from our friends, and also from the supplies so generously sent to the citizens generally, which were distributed at once, and, owing to the hurry and confusion then existing, without record.

We had notice of goods shipped us, that were received by the Chicago Relief and Aid Society, and distributed by them, But upon evidence that the goods were intended for the Fraternity, the Officers of the Society replaced the same.

If any of our friends fail to find their gifts recorded, they have the explanation here.

STATE OF MAINE.
BANGOR.
St. Andrews Lodge, No. 83, by J. H. Lynde, G. M., ...$100 00
LEWISTON.
Ashlar Lodge, No. 105, by H. H. Dickey, Treas., ...100 00
PORTLAND.
Portland Lodge, No. 1, by Benj. F. Andrews, W. M., ... 100 00
Ancient Landmark Lodge, No. 17, by Geo. W. Deering, ... 100 00
STANDISH.
Standish Lodge, No. 70, by Ira Berry, Gr. Sec'y, ... 50 00

Total amount received from Maine, ...$450 00

STATE OF NEW HAMPSHIRE.
CONCORD.

Craft, at Concord, by J. A. Harris, ----------------------------- $200 00

Total amount received from New Hampshire, ------------ $200 00

STATE OF MASSACHUSETTS.

The donations in the following list includes moneys sent from Massachusetts to Wisconsin and Michigan. It becomes impracticable, therefore, to credit to each particular Lodge the amount received for Chicago. We have, therefore, listed the total amount received by R. W. Charles H. Titus, Grand Secretary, viz:

M. W. GRAND LODGE OF MASSACHUSETTS,
  by Chas. H. Titus, Grand Secretary, ------ $1,000 00

ABINGTON.
John Cutler, by Chas H. Titus, Gr. Sec'y, ----------------------- 100 00

ATTLEBORO'.
Bristol Lodge, by Chas. H. Titus, Gr. Sec'y, --------------------- 200 00

BOSTON.
Germania Lodge, by Chas. H. Titus, Gr. Sec'y, ------------------ 25 00
Joseph Warren Lodge, by Charles H. Titus, Gr. Sec'y, ----------- 500 00
Aberdour Lodge, by Chas. H. Titus, Gr. Sec'y, ------------------ 180 00

BOSTON HIGHLANDS.
Washington Lodge, by Chas. H. Titus, Gr. Sec'y, --------------- 250 00

CHELSEA.
Star of Bethlehem Lodge, by Charles H. Titus, Gr. Sec'y, ---------- 18 00

DANVERS.
Mosaic Lodge, by Charles H. Titus, Gr. Sec'y, ------------------- 53 00

DEDHAM.
Constellation Lodge, U. D., by Charles H. Titus, Gr. Sec'y, -------- 53 00

DORCHESTER.
Union Lodge, by Charles H. Titus, Gr. Sec'y, ------------------- 100 00

EAST CAMBRIDGE.
Putnam Lodge, by Charles H. Titus, Gr. Sec'y, ------------------ 75 68

EVERETT.
Palestine Lodge, by Charles H. Titus, Gr. Sec'y, ---------------- 41 00

FALL RIVER.
Mount Hope Lodge, by Chas. H. Titus, Gr. Sec'y, --------------- 50 00

FITCHBURG.
Aurora Lodge, by Chas. H. Titus, Gr. Sec'y, --------------------- 152 00

GREENFIELD.
Republican Lodge, by Chas. H. Titus, Gr. Sec'y......................$ 50 00

HINGHAM.
Old Colony Lodge, by Chas. H. Titus, Gr. Sec'y.................. 300 00

HINSDALE.
Globe Lodge, by Chas. H. Titus, Gr. Sec'y,........................ 50 00

HUDSON.
Doric Lodge, by Charles H. Titus, Gr. Sec'y,...................... 100 00

HYANNIS.
Fraternal Lodge, by Charles H. Titus, Gr. Sec'y,.................. 100 00

IPSWICH.
John T. Heard Lodge, by Charles H. Titus, Gr. Sec'y,............. 100 00

JAMAICA PLAINS.
Eliot Lodge, by Chas. H. Titus, Gr. Sec'y,......................... 25 00

LOWELL.
Pentucket Lodge, by Charles H. Titus, Gr. Sec'y,................. 100 00
William North Lodge, by Chas. H. Titus, Gr. Sec'y,............... 100 00

MALDEN.
Mount Vernon Lodge, by Chas. H. Titus, Gr. Sec'y,............... 100 00

MANSFIELD.
Saint James Lodge, by Chas. H. Titus, Gr. Sec'y, ... 50 00

MARLBORO'.
United Brethern Lodge, by Chas. H. Titus, Gr. Sec'y,............. 110 00
United Brethern Lodge, by Chas. H. Titus, Gr. Sec'y,............. 5 00

MARION.
Pythagorian Lodge, by Charles H. Titus, Gr, Sec'y,............... 20 00

METHUEN.
John Hancock Lodge, by Charles H. Titus, Gr. Sec'y,.............. 11 00

NEW BEDFORD.
Eureka Lodge, by Chas. H. Titus, Gr. Sec'y,....................... 25 00
Star in the East Lodge, by Charles H. Titus, Gr. Sec'y,........... 50 00

NEWTONVILLE.
Dalhousie Lodge, by Charles H. Titus, Gr. Sec'y,.................. 100 00

NORTH ADAMS.
LaFayette Lodge, by Chas. H. Titus, Gr. Sec'y,.................... 127 00

NORTH EASTON.
Paul Dean Lodge, by Chas. H. Titus, Gr. Sec'y,.................... 50 00

OXFORD.
Oxford Lodge, by Charles H. Titus, Gr. Sec'y,----------------$ 5 00
PITTSVILLE.
Mystic Lodge, by Charles H. Titus, Gr. Sec'y,----------------- 172 00
PROVINCETOWN.
King Hiram Lodge, by Chas. H. Titus, Gr. Sec'y,--------------- 79 25
PLYMOUTH.
Plymouth Lodge, by Charles H. Titus, Gr. Sec'y,--------------- 200 00
Plymouth Lodge, by Charles H. Titus, Gr. Sec'y,--------------- 15 00
QUINCY.
Rural Lodge, by Chas. H. Titus, Gr. Sec'y,-------------------- 100 00
READING.
Good Samaritan Lodge, by Charles H. Titus, Gr. Sec'y,--------- 70 00
SHELBOURNE FALLS.
Mountain Lodge, by Chas. H. Titus, Gr. Sec'y,----------------- 25 00
SOMERSET.
Pioneer Lodge, by Charles H. Titus, Gr. Sec'y, --------------- 15 00
SOUTH ABINGDON.
Puritan Lodge, by Chas. H. Titus, Gr. Sec'y, ----------------- 60 00
SOUTHBRIDGE.
Quinebaug Lodge, by Chas. H. Titus, Gr. Sec'y,---------------- 33 00
SOUTH BOSTON.
Gate of the Temple Lodge, by Chas. H. Titus, Gr. Sec'y, ------ 100 00
Rabboni Lodge, by Chas. H. Titus, Gr. Sec'y,------------------ 50 00
SOUTHBORO'.
Saint Bernard Lodge, by Chas. H. Titus. Gr. Sec'y,------------ 41 00
SOUTH DEDHAM.
Orient Lodge, by Chas. H. Titus, Gr. Sec'y,------------------- 50 00
UXBRIDGE.
Solomon's Temple Lodge, by Charles H. Titus, Gr. Sec'y, ------ 108 50
WALTHAM.
Monitor Lodge, by Charles H. Titus, Gr. Sec'y,---------------- 100 00
Isaac Parker Lodge, by Chas. H. Titus, Gr. Sec'y,------------- 50 00
WAREHAM.
Social Harmony Lodge, by Charles H. Titus, Gr. Sec'y,--------- 35 00
WELLFLEET.
Adams Lodge, by Chas. H. Titus, Gr. Sec'y,-------------------- 50 00

WESTFIELD.
Mount Moriah Lodge, by Charles H. Titus, Gr. Sec'y, ...$ 20 00
WEST HARWICH.
Mount Horeb Lodge, by Charles H. Titus, Gr. Sec'y, ... 50 00

Total, ...$5,799 43
From this is deducted amount sent to Wisconsin and
    Michigan, viz.: .... 600 00—5,199 43
Being amount actually received from Bro. Titus, at Chicago.

In addition to this, the following contributions were received from Mass.:
CAMBRIDGE.
Amicable Lodge, by J. C. Wellington, Treas. $200 00
CHARLESTON.
King Solomon's Lodge, by G. P. Kettle, Treas., ... 100 00
HAVERHILL.
[NOTE.—Messrs. Pinkham & Sheldon, No. 128 Merrimack street, in a letter of advice, of Oct. 14, 1871, addressed to the Grand Master, state that they had forwarded a box of Clothing and Shoes. The goods were not delivered to this Board. Supposed to have been delivered to the Chicago Relief and Aid Society, and by them issued to the sufferers.]
PEABODY.
Jordan Lodge, by W. L. Gray, ... 100 00
PLYMOUTH.
Plymouth Lodge, by Chas. H. Titus, Gr. Sec'y, ... 3 28
WORCESTER.
Craft of Worcester, per T. E. St. John, D. D. G. M., in person,... 1,800 00

Horace A. Richardson, W. M. of Morning Star Lodge, Henry C. Willson, W. M. of Monticate Lodge, and James J. Russ, W. M. of Athelstan Lodge, were appointed a committee to receive the amounts contributed. The entire amount collected was $1,902, of which $102 was disbursed by Bro. St. John to needy brethern here, as per instructions of the donors. The remainder was paid to this Board.
    Total from Massachusetts, ...$7,402 71

The following extract from the proceedings of the Grand Lodge of Massachusetts, pp. 223, 224 and 225, will further explain the matter:

To M. W. Grand Master, William Sewall Gardner:
I herewith submit to you a full report of the contributions for Chicago, Wisconsin and Michigan, received by Recording Grand Secretary:
    Total amount received, ...$5,799 43

MASONIC BOARD OF RELIEF.

This amount has been deposited with the Grand Treasurer, and orders drawn upon him, as follows:

To M. W. DeWitt C. Cregier, Grand Master of Masons of Illinois, Chairman of Masonic Relief Committee: * * * * Drafts for the following amounts: $1,500, $2,100, $1,000 $200 and $399.43. In all $5,199.43.
To M. W. John W. Champlin, Grand Master of Masons in Michigan, Chairman, etc., $300 and $100. In all, $400.
To A. V. H. Carpenter, Chairman Masonic Relief Committee, Wisconsin, $200.

Total to Chicago,	$5,199 43
" " Michigan,	400 00
" " Wisconsin,	200 00
	$5,799 43

STATE OF RHODE ISLAND.
NEWPORT.

Newport R. A. Chapter, William G. Stephens,	$100 00
Total amount from Rhode Island	$100 00

STATE OF CONNECTICUT.
GEORGETOWN.

Ark Lodge, No. 39, David H. Miller, Sec'y,	$ 50 00

HARTFORD.

St. John's Lodge, No. 4, by Seth E. Marsh, W. M., and H. R. Morley, Sec'y,	100 00
St. John's Lodge, No. 4, by Seth E. Marsh, W. M., G. W. Tuller, W. M., and Geo. Lee, W. M., Committee	262 00
Hartford Lodge, No. 88, by G. W. Tuller, W. M.,	100 00
Hartford Lodge, No. 88, by Seth E. Marsh, W. M., G. W. Tuller, W. M., and Geo. Lee, W. M., Committee	262 00
Lafayette Lodge, No. 100, by Geo. Lee, W. M.,	100 00
Lafayette Lodge, No. 100, by Seth E. Marsh, W. M., G. W. Tuller, W. M., and Geo. Lee, W. M., Committee	262 00

NEW LONDON.

Brainard Lodge, No. 102, by P. C. Dumford,	100 00

WILMATIC.

Eastern Star Lodge, No. 44, by Van N. Austin, W. M.,	100 00

WINDSOR.

Washington Lodge, No. 70, by Jas. T. Templeton, W. M.,	50 00

The following list of donations were received through M. W. James L. Gould, Grand Master of Masons, in Connecticut:

BETHEL.
Eureka Lodge, No. 83, ... $ 25 00

BRIDGEPORT.
St. John's Lodge, No. 3, ... 108 34

COLLINSVILLE.
Village Lodge, No. 29, ... 15 00

EAST HAMPTON.
Lyon Lodge, No. 105, ... 12 00

JEWETT CITY.
Mount Vernon Lodge, No. 75, ... 26 00

MILFORD.
Ansantawae Lodge, No. 89, ... 25 00

MANCHESTER.
Manchester Lodge, No. 73, ... 118 00

NAUGATUCK.
Shepherd's Lodge, No. 78, ... 43 00

NEW BRITAIN.
Harmony Lodge, No. 20, ... 128 00

NEW CANAAN.
Harmony Lodge, No. 67, ... 20 00

NORFOLK.
Western Star Lodge, No. 37, ... 18 00

NORWALK.
St. John's Lodge, No. 6 .... 44 50

PLYMOUTH.
Union Lodge, No. 96, ... 27 00

WALLINGFORD.
Compass Lodge, No. 9, ... 62 00

WATERBURY.
Harmony Lodge, No. 42, ... 100 00
Continental Lodge, No. 76, ... 100 00

WATERTOWN.
Federal Lodge, No. 17, ... 25 00

WESTPORT.
Temple Lodge, No. 65, ... 59 28

WEST WINSTED.

St. Andrew's Lodge, No. 64,------------------------------ ------ $ 25 00

WOODBURY.

King Solomon Lodge, No. 7,-- 20 00
Total amount received from Bro. Gould $1.001.12, as follows:
Tools to the value of------------------------------------$462 44
Hats and Caps to the value of--------------------------- 52 50
Draft to the value of---------------------------------- 486 18

                                                         $1,001 12

Total amount from Connecticut,--------------------------------$2,387 12

STATE OF NEW YORK.

ADAMS.
Adams R. A. C., No. 205, by J. H. Miles--------------------------$ 50 00

ALBANY.
Masters' Lodge, No. 5, by J. H. Anthon, G. M.,-------------------- 500 00
One box clothing, per express, estimated value,------------------ 25 33

AUBURN.
St. Paul's Lodge, No. 124, by J. H. Anthon, G. M.,--------------- 100 00

BALDWINSVILLE.
Seneca River Lodge, No. 160, by H. J. Frazer, S. W.,------------ 178 00

BROCKPORT.
Monroe Lodge, No. 173, by John A. Getty, W. M.,---------------- 36 00

BROOKLYN.
Fortitude Lodge, No. 19, by J. H. Anthon, G. M.,---------------- 100 00
Hohenlinden Lodge, No. 56, by J. H. Anthon, G. M.,-------------- 50 00
Anglo Saxon Lodge, No. 137, by J. H. Anthon, G. M.,------------ 150 00
Marsh Lodge, No. 188, by J. H. Anthon, G. M.,------------------ 100 00
Baltic Lodge, No. 284, by J. H. Anthon, G. M.,------------------ 50 00
Montauk Lodge, No. 286, by J. H. Anthon, G. M.,---------------- 500 00
Schiller Lodge, No. 304, by J. H. Anthon, G. M.,---------------- 100 00
Corner Stone Lodge, No. 367, by J. H. Anthon, G. M.,----------- 50 00
Lexington Lodge, No. 310, by J. H. Anthon, G. M.,-------------- 50 00
Progressive Lodge, No. 354, by J. H. Anthon, G. M.,------------ 200 00
Long Island Lodge, No. 382, by J. H. Anthon, G. M.,------------ 50 00
Green Point Lodge, No. 403, by J. H. Anthon, G. M.,------------ 200 00
Star of Hope Lodge, No. 430, by J. H. Anthon, G. M.,----------- 100 00
Cassia Lodge, No. 445, by J. H. Anthon, G. M.,------------------ 100 00
Oltman's Lodge, No. 446, by J. H. Anthon, G. M.,---------------- 50 00
Yew Tree Lodge, No. 461, by J. H. Anthon, G. M.,---------------- 50 00

FINAL REPORT OF THE

Zeredatha Lodge, No. 483, by J. H. Anthon, G. M., ... $100 00
Nassau Lodge, No. 536, by J. H. Anthon, G. M., ... 100 00
Copernicus Lodge, No. 545, by J. H. Anthon, G. M., ... 158 00
Greenwood Lodge, No. 569, by J. H. Anthon, G. M., ... 100 00
Greenwood Lodge, No. 569, by J. H. Anthon, G. M., ... 6 00
Altair Lodge, No. 601, by Peter M. Borland, W. M., ... 150 00
Central Lodge, No. 631, by J. H. Anthon, G. M., ... 300 00
Euclid Lodge, No. 656, by J. H. Anthon, G. M., ... 100 00
Seawanhaka Lodge, No. 678, by J. H. Anthon, G. M., ... 100 00
Tuscan Lodge, No. 704, by J. H. Anthon, G. M., ... 50 00
Herder Lodge, No. 698, by J. H. Anthon, G. M., ... 50 00
Gate of Temple, R. A. Chapter, No. 208, by J. H. Anthon, G. M.,.. 50 00

BUFFALO.
Hiram Lodge, No. 105, by Wm. F. Rogers, W. M., ... 100 00
Washington Lodge, No. 240, by C. C. Cander, W. M., ... 200 00
Queen City, No. 358, by C. G. Fox, Secretary, ... 200 00
De Molay Lodge, No. 498, by J. E. Barnard, Secretary, ... 100 00

CALLICOON.
Callicoon Lodge, No. 521, by J. H. Anthon, G. M., ... 30 00

CHESTER.
Standard Lodge, No. 711, by J. H. Anthon, G. M., ... 38 00

CITY ISLAND.
Pelham Lodge, No. 712, by J. H. Anthon, G. M., ... 53 00

COLLEGE POINT.
College Point Masons, by J. H. Anthon, G. M., ... 52 00

COOPERSTOWN.
Ostego Lodge, No. 138, by J. H. Anthon, G. M., ... 195 50

CLYDE.
Clyde Lodge, No. 341, by Jno. Vandenberg, W. M., ... 25 00

DOVER PLAINS.
Dover Lodge, No. 666, by J. H. Anthon, G. M., ... 25 00

ELLENBURG.
Mount Hermon Lodge, No. 572, by J. H. Anthon, G. M., ... 50 00

EVAN'S MILLS.
Craft at Evan's Mills, by J. H. Anthon, G. M., ... 43 00

GREENPORT.
Peconic Lodge, No. 349, by J. H. Anthon, G. M., ... 25 00

GLOVERSVILLE.
Gloversville Lodge, No. 429, by J. H. Anthon, G. M., ... 300 00
Gloversville Lodge, No. 429, by J. H. Anthon, G. M., ... 153 00

MASONIC BOARD OF RELIEF. 53

HAMMONDSPORT.
Urbana Lodge, No. 459, by C. S. Bromwell, Secretary,........... $ 5 00
HOOSICK FALLS.
Van Rensselaer Lodge, No. 400, by J. H. Anthon, G. M.,.......... 132 00
HUDSON.
Hudson Lodge, No. 7, by J. H. Anthon, G. M.,................... 100 00
Aquilla Lodge, No. 700, by J. H. Anthon, G. M.,................ 50 00
JAMAICA.
Jamaica Lodge, No. 546, by J. H. Anthon, G. M.,................ 137 00
LOCKPORT.
Lockport Lodge, No. 73, by J. H. Anthon, G. M.,................ 100 00
LYONS.
Humanity Lodge, No. 406, by J. Willing, W. M.,................. 100 00
MAMARONECK.
Mamaro Lodge, No. 653, by J. H. Anthon, G. M.,................. 60 85
MARATHON.
Marathon Lodge, No. 438, by J. H. Anthon, G. M.,............... 49 00
MATTEAWAN.
Beacon Lodge, No. 283, by J. H. Anthon, G. M.,................. 50 00
MOTT HAVEN.
Gavel Lodge, No. 703, by J. H. Anthon, G. M.,.................. 50 00
MORRISANIA.
Lily Lodge, No. 342, by J. H. Anthon, G. M.,................... 50 00
MOUNT KISCO.
Kisco Lodge, No. 708, by J. H. Anthon, G. M.,.................. 25 00
NEW YORK CITY.
Independent R. A. Lodge, No. 2, by J. H. Anthon, G. M.,........ $ 500 00
Holland Lodge, No. 8, by J. H. Anthon, G. M.,.................. 1,070 00
Antiquity Lodge, No. 11, by J. H. Anthon, G. M.,............... 150 00
Prince of Orange Lodge, No. 16, by J. H. Anthon, G. M.,........ 166 00
Albion Lodge, No. 26, by J. H. Anthon, G. M.,.................. 250 00
Lafayette Lodge, No. 64, J. H. Anthon, G. M.,.................. 50 00
Mariners' Lodge, No. 67, by J. H. Anthon, G. M.,............... 60 00
Darcy Lodge No. 187, by J. H. Anthon, G. M.,................... 100 00
Lebanon Lodge, No. 191, by J. H. Anthon, G. M.,................ 150 00
Excelsior Lodge, No. 195, by J. H. Anthon, G. M.,.............. 150 00
York Lodge, No. 197, by Edwin Ganong, W. M.,................... 100 00
Templar Lodge, No. 203, by J. H. Anthon, G. M.,................ 173 00
Empire City Lodge, No. 206, by J. H. Anthon, G. M.,............ 200 00
Worth Lodge, No. 210, by J. H. Anthon, G. M.,.................. 150 00

Pacific Lodge, No. 233, by J. H. Anthon, G. M.,	$ 225 00
Keystone Lodge, No. 235, by J. H. Anthon, G. M.,	100 00
Hope Lodge, No. 244, by J. H. Anthon, G. M.,	350 00
Polar Star Lodge, No. 245, by J. H. Anthon, G. M.,	250 00
Mystic Tie Lodge, No. 272, by J. H. Anthon, G. M.,	100 00
Henry Clay Lodge, No. 277, by J. H. Anthon, G. M.,	1 00
King Solomon's Lodge, No. 279, by J. H. Anthon, G. M.,	150 00
Doric Lodge, No. 280, by J. H. Anthon, G. M.,	50 00
Acacia Lodge, No. 327, by J. H. Anthon, G. M.,	50 00
Hiram Lodge, No. 449, by J. H. Anthon, G. M.,	50 00
Kane Lodge, No. 454, by J. H. Anthon, G. M.,	180 00
Greenwich Lodge, No. 467, by J. H. Anthon, G. M.,	50 00
Ionic Lodge, No. 486, by J. H. Anthon, G. M.,	100 00
Corinthian Lodge, No. 488, by J. H. Anthon, G. M.,	218 00
Pyramid Lodge, No. 490, by Jno. Cook, Treasurer,	300 00
Humboldt Lodge, No. 512, by J. H. Anthon, G. M.,	100 00
Park Lodge, No. 516, by J. H. Anthon, G. M.,	100 00
Monitor Lodge, No. 528, by J. H. Anthon, G. M.,	50 00
Americus Lodge, No. 535, by J. H. Anthon, G. M.,	25 00
Gramercy Lodge, No. 537, by J. H. Anthon, G. M.,	250 00
St. Cecil Lodge, No. 568, by J. H. Anthon, G. M.,	100 00
Fessler Lodge, No. 576, by J. H. Anthon, G. M.,	142 50
Ivanhoe Lodge, No. 610, by J. H. Anthon, G. M.,	277 00
Scotia Lodge, No. 634, by J. H. Anthon, G. M.,	200 00
Cope Stone Lodge, No. 641, by J. H. Anthon, G. M.,	250 00
Daniel Carpenter Lodge, No. 643, by J. H. Anthon, G. M.,	100 00
True Craftsman's Lodge, No. 651, by J. H. Anthon, G. M.,	25 00
Republic Lodge, No. 690, by Gilbert R. Smith,	225 00

The actual amount contributed by Republic Lodge was $250.00. Twenty-five dollars had been disbursed to a needy brother, as per instruction of the donors, leaving $225.00 to be turned over to this Board.

Merchants' Lodge, No. 709, by J. H. Anthon, G. M.,	1,205 00
Wieland Lodge, U. D., by J. H. Anthon, G. M.,	195 00
W. J. Turner, of Crescent Lodge, No. 402, by J. H. Anthon, G. M.,	10 00
J. H. T., of Crescent Lodge, No. 402, by J. H. Anthon, G. M.,	5 00
J. F. Ferguson, of Kane Lodge, No. 454, by J. H. Anthon, G. M.,	50 00
G. Argentine, of Calvary Lodge, No. 59, Kansas, by J. H. Anthon, G. M.,	5 00
Masonic Quartette Club, by J. H. Anthon, G. M.,	25 00
E. W. Henry, U. S. N., by J. H. Anthon, G. M.,	10 00
James Wilson, U. S. N., by J. H. Anthon, G. M.,	10 00
Richey & Boniface, 122 Water St., by J. H. Anthon, G. M.,	100 00
Hoeg & Hurtevant and employees, 389 Broome St., by J. H. Anthon, G. M.	80 00

MASONIC BOARD OF RELIEF. 55

Davis & Corson, 39 Nassau St., by J. H. Anthon, G. M. ....$ 4 00
Isaac H. Brown, Sexton Grace Church, by J. H. Anthon, G. M....... 50 00
One box clothing, for women and children, from Alpha Chapter, No.
  1, O. E. S., through Bro. Robert Macoy. Value,...............222 10

NIAGARA FALLS.
Niagara Frontier Lodge, No. 132, by Jas. B. King, W. M........... 75 00

PEEKSKILL.
Cortland Lodge, No. 289, by J. H. Anthon, G. M................... 5 00

PORT RICHMOND.
Richmond Lodge, No. 66, by J. H. Anthon, G. M................... 25 00

POUGHKEEPSIE.
Poughkeepsie Lodge, No. 266, by J. H. Anthon, G. M.............. 100 00

RHINEBECK.
Rhinebeck Lodge, No. 432, by J. H. Anthon, G. M................. 27 00

RICHFIELD SPRINGS.
Richfield Springs Lodge, No. 482, by J. H. Anthon, G. M......... 150 00

ROCHESTER.
Craft of Rochester, by W. F. Holmes, Prest. M. B'd of Relief... 1000 00

RONDOUT.
Rondout Lodge, No. 343, by J. H. Anthon, G. M................... 100 00

SANDY HILL.
Sandy Hill Lodge, No. 372, by J. H. Anthon, G. M................ 50 00

SARATOGA SPRINGS.
Rising Sun Lodge, No. 108, by J. H. Anthon, G. M................ 50 00

SYRACUSE.
Joseph Seymour & Sons, ... 25 00

In addition to the above, the Brethren Seymour sent, through this Board, $25.00 to the I. O. of O. F., and a set of Jewels for a Lodge, Chapter and Commandery; which were, at their request, given by lot to Lincoln Park Lodge, No. 611, Corinthian Chapter, No. 69, and Apollo Commandery, No. 1.

TARRYTOWN.
Solomon's Lodge, No. 196, by J. H. Anthon, G. M................. 50 00
Solomon's Lodge, No. 196, by J. H. Anthon, G. M................. 85 00
Solomon's Lodge, No. 196, by J. H. Anthon, G. M................. 5 00

TOTTENVILLE.
W. A. Seacor, of Huguenot Lodge, by J. H. Anthon, G. M.......... 15 00

TROY.
King Solomon's Primitive Lodge, No. 91, by J. H. Anthon, G. M.. 100 00

TUCKAHOE.
Marble Lodge, No. 702, by J. H. Anthon, G. M.................... 50 00

WAPPINGER'S FALLS.
Wappinger's Falls Lodge, No. 671, by J. H. Anthon, G. M........$200 00
WHITE PLAINS.
White Plains Lodge, No. 473, by J. H. Anthon, G. M............. 64 00
YONKERS.
Rising Star Lodge, No. 450, by J. H. Anthon, G. M. 650 00

Total amount received from New York,...............$18,636 28

At the request of the President of this Board, M. W. John H. Anthon, G. M., purchased a bill of dry goods to the amount of $1,052.55, of Messrs. Champion & Stewart, No. 831 Broadway, New York, who very generously made a deduction amounting to $52.55. As the goods are credited on our books at a valuation of $1,000.00, this acknowledgement is deemed proper.

STATE OF NEW JERSEY.
ABSECOM.
Trinity Lodge, No. 79, by W. E. Pine, G. M................. ....$100 00
ARMANDALE.
Stewart Lodge, No. 34, by W. E. Pine, G. M...................... 25 00
BELVIDERE.
J. B. Woodward, of Lodge No. 13, by W. E. Pine, G. M.......... 1 00
BERGEN.
Bergen Lodge, No. 47, by W. E. Pine, G. M...................... 11 50
BERGEN POINT.
Bayonne Lodge, No. 99, by W. E. Pine, G. M..................... 20 00
BELLEVILLE.
Belleville Lodge, No. 108, by J. H. Wisschusen, Treas., ... 25 00
BEVERLY.
Beverly Lodge, No. 107, by W. E. Pine, G. M. 32 00
BLOOMFIELD.
Bloomfield Lodge, No. 40, by W. E. Pine, G. M................... 106 00
BORDENTOWN.
Mount Moriah Lodge, No. 28, by W. E. Pine, G. M............... 50 00
BURLINGTON.
Burlington Lodge, No. 32, by Wilber Watts, W. M............... 100 00
BOONTON.
Arcana Lodge, No. 60, by W. E. Pine, G. M..................... 25 00
CAMDEN.
Mozart Lodge, No. 121, by W. E. Pine, G. M.................... 50 00

MASONIC BOARD OF RELIEF.   57

DECKERTOWN.
Samaritan Lodge, No. 98, by W. E. Pine, G. M., ... $ 57 00
DOVER.
Acacia Lodge, No. 20, by W. E. Pine, G. M., ... 200 00
ELIZABETH.
Washington Lodge, No. 33, by W. E. Pine, G. M., ... 100 00
ELIZABETHPORT.
Essex Lodge, No. 49, by W. E. Pine, G. M., ... 25 00
FREEHOLD.
Olive Branch Lodge, No. 16, by W. E. Pine, G. M., ... 10 00
GLASSBORO'.
Glassboro' Lodge, No. 85, by W. E. Pine, G. M., ... 25 00
GLOUCESTER CITY.
Cloud Lodge, No. 101, by W. E. Pine, G. M., ... 37 00
HOBOKEN.
Hudson Lodge, No. 71, by Wm. Hartung, Sec'y, ... 50 00
JERSEY CITY.
Hiram Lodge, No. 17, by W. E. Pine, G. M., ... 250 00
Enterprise Lodge, No. 48, by W. E. Pine, G. M., ... 100 00
Teutonia Lodge, No. 72, by W. E. Pine, G. M., ... 50 00
Jersey City Lodge, No. 74, by W. E. Pine, G. M., ... 100 00
Rising Star Lodge, No. 109, by W. E. Pine, G. M., ... 50 00
LAFAYETTE.
Amity Lodge, No. 103, by W. E. Pine, G. M., ... 50 00
MADISON.
Madison Lodge, No. 93, by W. E. Pine, G. M., ... 216 00
Madison Lodge, No. 93, by W. E. Pine, G. M., ... 20 00
MAURICETOWN.
Neptune Lodge, No. 75, by W. E. Pine, G. M., ... 25 00
MERCHANTVILLE.
Merchantville Lodge, No. 119, by W. E. Pine, G. M., ... 35 50
MORRISTOWN.
Cincinnati Lodge, No. 3, by W. E. Pine, G. M., ... 100 00
NEWARK.
Newark Lodge, No. 7, by W. E. Pine, G. M., ... 250 00
Eureka Lodge, No. 39, by W. E. Pine, G. M., ... 100 00
Oriental Lodge, No. 51, by W. E. Pine, G. M., ... 100 00
Kane Lodge, No. 55, by Wm. D. Kinney, ... 100 00
Schiller Lodge, No. 66, by W. E. Pine, G. M., ... 100 00

Bro. Joseph Hensler of Lodge No. 66, by W. E. Pine, G. M., ...$100 00
Cosmos Lodge, No. 106, by W. E. Pine, G. M., ... 50 00
Pythagoras Lodge, No. 118, by W. E. Pine, G. M., ... 35 00

NEW BRUNSWICK.
Union Lodge, No. 19, by W. E. Pine, G. M., ... 50 00
Palestine Lodge, No. 111, by W. E. Pine, G. M., ... 25 00

NEW EGYPT.
Pyramid Lodge, No. 92, by W. E. Pine, G. M., ... 25 00

ORANGE.
T. O. Ayers, of Lodge No. 11, by W. E. Pine, G. M., ... 50 00

PASSAIC.
Passaic Lodge, No. 67, by W. E. Pine, G. M., ... 55 00

PATTERSON.
Benevolent Lodge, No. 45, by W. E. Pine, G. M., ... 100 00
Falls City Lodge, No. 82, by W. E. Pine, G. M., ... 50 00
Ivanhoe Lodge, No. 88, by W. E. Pine, G. M., ... 100 00
Humboldt Lodge, No. 114, by W. E. Pine, G. M., ... 52 50

PERTH AMBOY.
Raritan Lodge, No. 61, by W. E. Pine, G. M., ... 43 50

PHILLIPSBURG.
Delaware Lodge, No. 52, by W. E. Pine, G. M., ... 50 00

PRINCETON.
Princeton Lodge, No. 38, by W. E. Pine, G. M., ... 10 00

RAHWAY.
Lafayette Lodge, No. 27, by W. E. Pine, G. M., ... 100 00

RED BANK,
Mystic Brotherhood Lodge, No. 21, by W. E. Pine, G. M., ... 75 00

SEAVILLE.
Cannon Lodge, No. 104, by W. E. Pine, G. M., ... 38 00

SOUTH AMBOY.
St. Stephen's Lodge, No. 63, by W. E. Pine, G. M., ... 50 00

TOM'S RIVER.
Harmony Lodge, No. 18, by W. E. Pine, G. M., ... 50 00

TRENTON.
Trenton Lodge, No. 5, by W. E. Pine, G. M., ... 100 00
Mercer Lodge, No. 50, by W. E. Pine, G. M., ... 50 00
Ashlar Lodge, No. 76, by W. E. Pine, G. M., ... 50 00
Column Lodge, No. 120, by W. E. Pine, G. M., ... 50 00

TUCKERTON.
Tuckerton Lodge, No. 4, by W. E. Pine, G. M...................$ 15 00
UNION.
Mystic Tie Lodge, No. 123, by W. E. Pine, G. M.,............... 20 00
VINCENTOWN.
Central Lodge, No. 44, by W. E. Pine, G. M.,.................. 25 00
VINELAND.
Vineland Lodge, No. 69, by W. E. Pine, G. M.,................. 20 00
WEST HOBOKEN.
Doric Lodge, No. 86, by W. E. Pine, G. M.,.................... 50 00
WOODBRIDGE.
Americus Lodge, No. 83, by W. E. Pine, G. M.,................. 62 00
LOCATION UNKNOWN.
Union R. A. C., No. 7, by W. E. Pine, G. M................... 100 00
Collected by G. E. B., by W. E. Pine, G. M., ... '94 20

Total amount received from New Jersey,................ $4,441 20

Bro. August Scharsberger, of Hudson Lodge, No. 71, Hoboken, sent $46.05 through Bro. Wm. Hartung, Sec'y of No. 71, with the request that the amount be equally divided between the two most destitute members of Lessing Lodge, No. 557, Chicago. The amount was handed to the Master of No. 557, together with the instruction of the donor.

STATE OF PENNSYLVANIA.

M. W. GRAND LODGE OF PENN., by John Thomson, Gr. Sec'y,...$1,000 00
ALTOONA.
Mountain Lodge, No. 281, by John Thomson, Gr. Sec'y........... 100 00
ALLENTOWN.
Allen R. A. C., No. 203, by John Thomson, Gr. Sec'y........... 25 00
ASHLAND.
Ashland Lodge, No. 294, by John Thomson, Gr. Sec'y,........... 25 00
ATHENS.
Rural Amity Lodge, No. 70, by John Thomson, Gr. Sec'y,........ 100 00
BIRMINGHAM.
Monongahela Lodge, No. 269, by John Thomson, Gr. Sec'y,....... 50 00
BLAIRSVILLE.
Acacia Lodge, No. 355, by John Thomson, Gr. Sec'y............. 10 00
CANTON.
Canton Lodge, No. 415, by John Thomson, Gr. Sec'y,............ 10 00

CATAWISSA.
Catawissa Lodge, No. 349, by John Thomson, Gr. Sec'y,..........$ 20 00
CLEARFIELD.
Clearfield Lodge, No. 314, by John Thomson, Gr. Sec'y,............ 25 00
COATSVILLE.
Goddard Lodge, No. 383, by John Thomson, Gr. Sec'y,............ 20 00
COCHRANSVILLE.
Skerrett Lodge, No. 343, by John Thomson, Gr. Sec'y,............ 30 00
COLUMBIA.
Columbia Lodge, No. 286, by John Thomson, Gr. Sec'y,............ 75 00
CONDERSPORT.
Eulalia Lodge, No. 342, by John Thomson, Gr. Sec'y,.............. 50 00
CONSHOHOCKEN.
Fritz Lodge, No. 420, by John Thomson, Gr. Sec'y,.............. 50 00
CRESSONA.
Cressona Lodge, No. 426, by John Thomson, Gr. Sec'y,............ 20 00
DARLINGTON.
Meridian Lodge, No. 411, by John Thomson, Gr. Sec'y,............ 10 00
DOYLESTOWN.
Doylestown Lodge No. 245, by John Thomson, Gr. Sec'y,.......... 100 00
DUSHORE.
Dushore Lodge, No. 387, by John Thomson, Gr. Sec'y,............ 20 00
EASTON.
Easton Lodge, No. 152, by John Thomson, Gr. Sec'y,............ 50 00
EBENSBURG.'
Summit Lodge, No. 312, by John Thomson, Gr. Sec'y,............ 5 00
ELYSBURG.
Elysburg Lodge, No. 414, by John Thomson, Gr. Sec'y,............ 25 00
ERIE.
Tyrian Lodge, No. 362, by R. M. Moore, Sec'y,.................... 100 00
Perry Lodge, No. 392, by F. T. Longstreet, Sec'y,.................. 50 00
FACTORYVILLE.
Factoryville Lodge, No. 341, by John Thomson Gr. Sec'y,.......... 50 00
FREMONT.
Swatara Lodge, No. 267, by John Thomson Gr. Sec'y,............ 50 00
FORT WASHINGTON.
Fort Washington Lodge, No. 408, by John Thomson, Gr. Sec'y,.... 25 00

FRANKFORD.
Frankford Lodge, No. 292, by John Thomson, Gr. Sec'y, ... $ 50 00

GERMANTOWN.
Mitchell Lodge, No. 296, by John Thomson, Gr. Sec'y, ... 150 00

GREENSBURG.
Philanthropy Lodge, No. 225, by John Thomson, Gr. Sec'y, ... 100 00

GREENFIELD.
Monongahela Valley Lodge, No. 461, by John Thomson, Gr. Sec'y,.. 7 50

HAMBURG.
Vaux Lodge, No. 406, by John Thomson, Gr. Sec'y, ... 12 00

HATBORO'.
W. K. Bray Lodge, No. 410, by John Thomson, Gr. Sec'y, ... 25 00

HARMONY.
Harmony Lodge, No. 429, by John Thomson, Gr. Sec'y, ... 30 00

HARRISBURG.
Perseverance Lodge, No. 21, by John Thomson, Gr. Sec'y, ... 175 00
Robert Burns Lodge, No. 464, by John Thomson, Gr. Sec'y,........ 135 00

HAZELTON.
Hazel Lodge, No. 327, by John Thomson, Gr. Sec'y, ... 100 00

HOLLIDAYSBURG.
Juniata Lodge, No. 282, by John Thomson, Gr. Sec'y, ... 50 00

HUNTINGTON.
Mount Moriah Lodge, No. 300, by John Thomson, Gr. Sec'y, ... 25 00

HYDE PARK.
Hyde Park Lodge, No. 339, by John Thomson, Gr. Sec'y, ... 50 00

INDIANA.
Indiana Lodge, No. 313, by John Thomson, Gr. Sec'y, ... 10 00

JACKSON.
Freedom Lodge, No. 328, by John Thomson, Gr. Sec'y, ... 24 85

JENKINTOWN.
Friendship Lodge, No. 400, by John Thomson, Gr. Sec'y, ... 25 00

JOHNSTOWN.
Cambria Lodge, No. 278, by John Thomson, Gr. Sec'y, ... 50 00

KENSINGTON.
Kensington Lodge, No. 211, by John Thomson, Gr. Sec'y, ... 100 00
Athelstan Lodge, No. 482, by John Thomson, Gr. Sec'y, ... 100 00

KIRKWOOD.
Colerain Lodge, No. 417, by John Thomson, Gr. Sec'y, ... 5 00

KITTANING.
Kittaning Lodge, No. 244, by John Thomson, Gr. Sec'y, ... $ 50 00

LANCASTER.
Lamberton Lodge, No. 476, by George K. Reed, W. M., ... 100 00
Lodge No. 43, by George K. Reed, W. M., ... 300 00

LEBANON.
Mount Lebanon Lodge, No. 226, by John Thomson, Gr. Sec'y, ... 50 00

LEWISBURG.
Charity Lodge, No. 144, by J. A. Kline, W. M., ... 100 00

MAHONY CITY.
Mahony City Lodge, No. 357, by John Thomson, Gr. Sec'y, ... 25 00

MANAYUNK.
Roxborough Lodge, No. 135, by John Thomson, Gr. Sec'y, ... 25 00

McKEESPORT.
Alliquippa Lodge, No. 375, by John Thomson, Gr. Sec'y, ... 25 00

MEADVILLE.
Crawford Lodge, No. 234, by John Thomson, Gr. Sec'y, ... 50 00

MILFORD.
Milford Lodge, No. 344, by John Thomson, Gr. Sec'y, ... 25 00

MILTON.
Milton Lodge, No. 256, by John Thomson, Gr. Sec'y, ... 15 00

MINERSVILLE.
Minersville Lodge, No. 222, by John Thomson, Gr. Sec'y, ... 25 00

MONTOURSVILLE.
Eureka Lodge, No. 335, by John Thomson, Gr. Sec'y, ... 10 00

MORGANTOWN.
Lodge No. 489, by John Thomson, Gr. Sec'y, ... 25 00

MOUNT CARMEL.
Mount Carmel Lodge, No. 378, by John Thomson, Gr. Sec'y, ... 16 00

NEW BRIGHTON.
Union Lodge, No. 259, by John Thomson, Gr. Sec'y, ... 35 00

NEWCASTLE.
Three Master Masons of Newcastle, by John Thomson, Gr. Sec'y, ... 200 80

NORRISTOWN.
Charity Lodge, No. 190, by John Thomson, Gr. Sec'y, ... 25 00

NORTHEAST.
Lodge No. 399, by John Thomson, Gr. Sec'y, ... 100 00

MASONIC BOARD OF RELIEF. 63

ORRSTOWN.

Orrstown Lodge, No. 262, by John Thomson, Gr. Sec'y,..........$ 20 00

ORWIGSBURG.

Schuylkill Lodge, No. 138, by John Thomson, Gr. Sec'y,.......... 50 00

PHILADELPHIA.

Lodge No. 2, by John Thomson, Gr. Sec'y,...................... 100 00
Lodge No. 3, by John Thomson, Gr. Sec'y,...................... 100 00
Lodge No. 9, by John Thomson, Gr. Sec'y, ... 50 00
Lodge No. 51, by John Thomson, Gr. Sec'y,..................... 100 00
Harmony Lodge, No. 52, by John Thomson, Gr, Sec'y,............ 50 00
Concordia Lodge, No. 67, by John Thomson, Gr. Sec'y,.......... 100 00
Solomon's Lodge, No. 114, by John Thomson, Gr. Sec'y,......... 200 00
Phœnix Lodge, No, 130, by John Thomson, Gr. Sec'y,............ 250 00
Meridian Sun Lodge, No. 158, by John Thomson, Gr. Sec'y,...... 100 00
Eastern Star Lodge, No. 186, by John Thomson, Gr. Sec'y,...... 350 00
Integrity Lodge, No. 187, by John Thomson, Gr. Sec'y,......... 100 00
Girard Lodge, No. 214, by John Thomson, Gr. Sec'y,............ 100 00
Shekinah Lodge, No. 246, by Alfred T. Jones, Sec'y,........... 500 00
Melita Lodge, No. 295, by John Thomson, Gr. Sec'y,............ 50 00
Corinthian Lodge, No. 368, by John Thomson, Gr. Sec'y,........ 100 00
Pennsylvania Lodge, No. 380, by John Thomson, Gr, Sec'y,...... 50 00
Apollo Lodge, No. 386, by John Thomson, Gr. Sec'y,............ 100 00
Vaux Lodge, No. 393, by John Thomson, Gr. Sec'y,.............. 100 00
Perkins Lodge, No. 402, by John Thomson, Gr. Sec'y,........... 50 00
Potter Lodge, No. 441, by John Thomson, Gr. Sec'y,............ 100 00
Philo Lodge, No. 444, by John Thomson, Gr. Sec'y,............. 25 00
Ivanhoe Lodge, No. 449, by John Thomson, Gr. Sec'y,........... 102 00
Stephen Girard Lodge, No. 450, by John Thomson, Gr. Sec'y,.... 50 00
Welcome Lodge, No. 453, by John Thomson, Gr. Sec'y,........... 50 00
Palestine Lodge, No. 470, by John Thomson, Gr. Sec'y,......... 100 00
St. Paul's Lodge, No. 481, by John Thomson, Gr. Sec'y,........ 50 00
R. A. Lamberton Lodge, No. 487, by John Thomson, Gr. Sec'y,... 30 00
Excelsior Lodge, No. 491, by John Thomson, Gr. Sec'y,......... 50 00
W. C. Hamilton Lodge, No. 500, by John Thomson, Gr. Sec'y,.... 100 00
Columbia R. A. C., No. 91, by John Thomson, Gr. Sec'y,........ 100 00
Philad. Council R. & S. Masters, No. 11, by John Thomson, Gr. Sec'y, 100 00
J. B. Clow, by J. V. Le Moyne,................................ 50 00

PHILLIPSBURG.

Moshannon Lodge, No. 391, by John Thomson, Gr. Sec'y,......... 25 00

PINE GROVE.

Pine Grove Lodge, No. 409, by John Thomson, Gr. Sec'y,........ 20 00

PITTSBURGH.

St. John's Lodge, No. 219, by D. B. Roberts, Sec'y,.................$500 00
Solomon's Lodge, No. 251, by John Thomson, Gr. Sec'y,............ 50 00
Pittsburgh Lodge, No. 484, by John Thomson, Gr. Sec'y,........... 50 00

PITTSTON.

St. John's Lodge, No. 233, by John Thomson, Gr. Sec'y,........... 50 00

READING.

Lodge No. 62, by John Thomson, Gr. Sec'y,....................... 50 00
Chandler Lodge, No. 227, by John Thomson, Gr. Sec'y,............ 50 00
Teutonia Lodge, No. 367, by John Thomson, Gr. Sec'y,............ 54 00
St. John Lodge, No. 435, by John Thomson, Gr. Sec'y,............. 50 00

ROCHESTER.

Rochester Lodge, No. 229, by John Thomson, Gr. Sec'y,........... 50 00

SANDY LAKE.

Lake Lodge, No. 434, by John Thomson, Gr. Sec'y,................ 50 00

SCHUYLKILL HAVEN.

Page Lodge, No. 270, by John Thomson, Gr. Sec'y,................ 25 00

SHAMOKIN.

Shamokin Lodge, No. 255, by John Thomson, Gr. Sec'y,........... 15 00

SMETHPORT.

McKean Lodge, No. 388, by John Thomson, Gr. Sec'y,............ 10 00

STROUDSBURG.

Barger Lodge, No. 325, by John Thomson, Gr. Sec'y,.............. 25 00

SUNBURY.

Lodge No. 22, by John Thomson, Gr. Sec'y,...................... 25 00

SUSQUEHANNA DEPOT.

Canawacta Lodge, No. 360, by John Thomson, Gr. Sec'y,.......... 50 00

TAMAQUA.

Tamaqua Lodge, No. 238, by John Thomson, Gr. Sec'y,............ 50 00

THOMPSONTOWN.

Lamberton Lodge, No. 371, by John Thomson, Gr. Sec'y,.......... 30 00

TIDEOUTE.

Temple Lodge, No. 412, by John Thomson, Gr. Sec'y,.............. 25 00

TITUSVILLE.

Oil Creek Lodge, No. 303, by John Thomson, Gr. Sec'y,........... 100 00

UPPER UWCHLAN.

Mount Pickering Lodge, No. 446, by John Thomson, Gr. Sec'y,.... 25 00

WATSONTOWN.
Watsontown Lodge, No. 401, by John Thomson, Gr. Sec'y, ... $ 25 00

WAYNESVILLE.
Howell Lodge, No. 405, by John Thomson, Gr. Sec'y, ... 10 00

WILLIAMSPORT.
Williamsport Lodge, No. 106, by John Thomson, Gr. Sec'y, ... 50 00

WOMELSDORF.
Williamson Lodge, No. 307, by John Thomson, Gr. Sec'y, ... 25 00

WHITE HAVEN.
Laurel Lodge, No. 467, by John Thomson, Gr. Sec'y, ... 20 00

YORK.
York Lodge, No. 266, by John Thomson, Gr. Sec'y, ... 50 00

Total amount received from Pennsylvania, ... $9,607 15

STATE OF MARYLAND.

BALTIMORE.
Cassia Lodge, No. 45, by J. H. Medairy, Gr. Sec'y, ... 16 00
Monumental Lodge, No. 96, by George L. Horn, J. W., ... 28 50
One Case Boots and Shoes (donor unknown), estimated value, ... 36 00

DENTON.
Temple Lodge, No. 128, by J. H. Medairy, Gr. Sec'y, ... 6 00

Total amount received from Maryland, ... $86 50

In response to an address issued to the Masonic Lodges of Maryland by the Grand Master, M. W. John H. B. Latrobe, contributions were received by the Grand Treasurer, amounting to $3,456.62, for the sufferers by the fires at Chicago, in Michigan and Wisconsin; to be equally divided between the three suffering districts. How this money was disposed of will be explained in the following extracts from the correspondence.

Extract from letter of M. W. H. L. Palmer, G. M., of Wisconsin, to the M. W. G. Master, of Maryland, acknowledging receipt of $1,152.21: * * * * * "The number of Masons who suffered by the fires in our State is limited, and the fund raised here, with some additions heretofore made to it from abroad, is ample for their relief. * * * If you will pardon me for the suggestion, I think the fund designed for Wisconsin is more needed in Chicago." * * * *

Extract from letter of the President of this Board, to the M. W. G. Master of Maryland, acknowledging the receipt of $2,304.62: * * * * "You observe that the contributions of the Masons of Maryland is for the benefit of the sufferers *generally* by the great fire. I desire to say, M. W. Sir, that all money coming to our Board is disbursed to *Masons only*, sufferers by the fire. As we have no means of reaching the masses, I am of the opinion that the amount forwarded by you should be handed over to the Chicago Relief and Aid Society." * * * * *

Extract from letter of President of this Board, to the M. W. G. Master of Maryland: * * * * * "Pursuant to your instructions, I have placed in the hands of the Chicago Relief and Aid Society the certificate of deposit for $2,304.62, contributed by our beloved Brethren of your jurisdiction to the sufferers *generally* by the late disastrous conflagration in our city." * * *

CHICAGO RELIEF AND AID SOCIETY,
Standard Hall, Cor. Michigan Avenue and 13th Street,
CHICAGO, JANUARY 18TH, 1872.

DEWITT C. CREGIER, ESQ., *Pres't and G. M. of Masons in Illinois:*

DEAR SIR: Your valued favor of the 12th inst. addressed to our Chairman, Mr. Dexter, with your remittance of $2,304.62, for benefit of our sufferers by fire, has been received, and is most gratefully acknowledged.

To your brother Masons of the State of Maryland, we desire to return our heartfelt thanks for this truly munificent gift, and this Society, as almoners of this great charity, also tender to your Board their appreciation of this handsome addition to the Relief Fund, on which some ten thousand families are even yet dependent for their partial or entire support. In a future publication of our cash donations, this good gift will appear.

Yours, very truly,
GEORGE M. PULLMAN.
C. G. HAMMOND, *Treasurer.*

STATE OF VIRGINIA.

FORT MONROE.

Craft of Fort Monroe, by W. E. Prescott and Jos. G. Fulton, Com.. $77 00
St. Johns R. A. C., No. 57, by W. E. Prescott and J. G. Fulton, Com., 40 00

Total amount received form Virginia, ...$117 00

DISTRICT OF COLUMBIA.

WASHINGTON.

Craft of Washington and District of Columbia, by C. F. Stansbury,
G. M., C. W. Franzonie, R. Ball, N. B. Fugett and W. A.
Short, Committee,----------------------------------$2,868 40
This amount was delivered by the entire Committee, in person.
Craft of Washington and District of Columbia, by C. F. Stansbury, G. M.,------------------------------------- 153 90

Total amount received from District of Columbia........$3,022 30

The total amount contributed by the Craft of the District of
Columbia was ---------------------------------------$3,334 90
Amount sent to Chicago was------------------------$3,022 30
Amount distributed to Chicago sufferers in Washington,
and expenses of concert, collection, etc., was------ 312 60
———$3,334 90

STATE OF SOUTH CAROLINA.

COLUMBIA.

Richland Lodge, No. 39, by G. J. Berg, Sec'y, ----------------- $25 00

Total amount received from South Carolina,------------ $25 00

STATE OF LOUISIANA.

Craft of Louisiana, by Samuel M. Todd, G. M.,----------------$400 00

Total amount received from Louisiana, ---------------$400 00

STATE OF OHIO.

CHILLICOTHE.
Sciota Lodge, No. 6, by Gilbert R. Smith,-------------------- $100 00

GALION.
Galion Lodge, No. 414, by Wm. Rogers,------------------------ 100 00

IRONTON.
Lawrence Lodge, No. — by D. W. Vogelson, W. M.,-- --------- 100 00

MILAN.
* Eureka Lodge, No. 69, by Geo. M. Dickson, W. M.,------------ 20 00

MOUNT VERNON.
Mount Zion Lodge, No. 9, by J. M. Burr,---------------------- 100 00
Clinton R. A. C., No. 26, by J. M. Burr, W. M.,--------------- 50 00
Clinton Commandery, K. T., by J. M. Burr, W. M.,------------- 50 00

SANDUSKY.
Perseverance Lodge, No. 329, by Jos. F. Kilby, Sec'y,--------- 104 00

YOUNGSTOWN.
Western Star Lodge, No. 20, per Express--------------------
Youngstown R. A. C., No. 93, per Express,------------------
Mahoning Council, No. 45, per Express,--------------------- } 75 00
St. John's Commandery, K. T., per Express, ----------------

Total amount received from Ohio,--------:------------ $699 00

* See Milan, Illinois, page 77.

STATE OF INDIANA.

Grand Council of Royal and Select Masters, by Martin H. Rice, G. M., ... $200 00

CROWN POINT.
Lincoln R. A. C., No. 53, by M. M. Stoltz, Sec'y, ... 25 00

EVANSVILLE.
Evansville Lodge, No. 64, by E. P. Elliott, Sec'y, ... 200 00

INDIANAPOLIS.
Marion Lodge, No. 35, by J. G. Waters, Sec'y, ... 100 00
Mystic Tie Lodge, No. 398, by John Cavin, W. M., ... 100 00

JEFFERSONVILLE.
Jeffersonville Lodge, No. 340, per Express 200 00

LOGANSPORT.
Orient Lodge, No. 272, by Sol. Fisher, Sec'y, ... 100 00

MORRISTOWN.
Morristown Lodge, No. 193, by Martin H. Rice, G. M., ... 15 00

NEW ALBANY.
New Albany Lodge, No. 39, by G. H. Devol and H. J. Kreamer,.. 100 00

ORLEANS.
Orleans Lodge, No. 153, by John Chenowith, Treas., ... 25 00

TERRE HAUTE.
Members of Terre Haute Lodge, No. 19, at Melrose, Illinois, by L. B. McClure, ... 4 00

Total amount received from Indiana, ... $1,069 00

STATE OF ILLINOIS.

ALBANY.
Albany Lodge, No. 566, by R. N. Brewer, Sec'y pro tem., ... $25 00

ALBION.
Hermitage Lodge, No. 356, by A. B. Mathews, Sec'y, ... 25 00

ALEDO.
Aledo Lodge, No. 252, by M. L. Marsh, Sec'y, ... 25 00

AMBOY.
Illinois Central Lodge, No. 178, by A. H. Wooster, W. M., ... 90 00

ANNAWAN.
Annawan Lodge, No. 433, by S. L. Andrews, Treas., ... 25 00

APPLE RIVER.
Apple River Lodge, No. 548, by F. H. Maynard, Sec'y, ... 25 00

AROMA.
Aroma Lodge, No. 378, by F. H. Brooks, ---------------------- $ 10 00

ARLINGTON.
Levi Lusk Lodge, No. 270, by R. B. Van Law, ----------------- 15 00

ATLANTA.
Atlanta Lodge, No. 163, by S. D. Fisher, Sec'y, ---------------- 25 00

AUGUSTA.
Craft of Augusta, by H. G. Dearborn, ------------------------- 25 00

AURORA.
Jerusalem Temple Lodge, No. 90, by Samuel Hoyles, W. M., ----- 100 00
Aurora Lodge No. 254, by C. Zimmer, Sec'y, ------------------ 50 00

AVON.
Avon Harmony Lodge, No. 253, by Oliver Crissey, W. M., -------- 23 50

BELLVILLE.
St. Clair Lodge, No. 24, by John Henzelman, ------------------- 100 00
Archimedes Lodge, No. 377, by C. Stephani, W. M., ------------ 50 00

BEMENT.
Bement Lodge, No. 365, by Chas. F. Tenney, W. M., ----------- 116 00

BLOOMFIELD.
Bloomfield Lodge, No. 148, by P. Calvin, Sec'y, ---------------- 25 00

BLOOMINGTON.
Mozart Lodge, No. 656, by D. Winter, Sec'y, ------------------ 50 00

BRIGHTON.
Hibbard Lodge, No. 249, by N. W. Waldo, Sec'y, --------------- 50 00

BUCKLEY.
Buckley Lodge, No. 634, by J. G. McClave, S. W., ------------- 50 00

BUNKER HILL.
Bunker Hill Lodge, No. 151, by F. W. Cross, W. M., ----------- 50 00
Bunker Hill Lodge, No. 151, by F. J. Hedley, Sec'y, ----------- 25 00

BURNT PRAIRIE.
Burnt Prairie Lodge, No. 668, by C. F. Chaefer, --------------- 10 00

BUSHNELL.
T. J. Pickett Lodge, No. 307, by W. J. Frisbee, W. M., --------- 77 15

BUTLER.
Butler Lodge No. 459, by Geo. W. Brown, Sec'y, --------------- 33 00

BYRON.
Byron Lodge, No. 274, by H. Kohn, of Chicago, -------------- 34 50

CAIRO.
Cairo Lodge, No. 237, by W. B. Kavey, J. W., ...$ 25 00
CANTON.
Morning Star Lodge, No. 30, by J. C. Brinkerhoff, ... 100 00
CAPRON.
One box Clothing, donors unknown, estimated value, ... 36 75
CARLINSVILLE.
Mount Nebo Lodge, No. 76, by S. Thompson Corn, Sec'y,......... 10 00
CARMAGO.
Carmago Lodge No, 440, by Geo. C. Hill, Treas.,............... 39 00
CARROLTON.
Carrolton Lodge, No. 50, by C. H. Kelley, S. W., ... 50 00
CATLIN.
Catlin Lodge, No. 285, by S. R. Tilton, Sec'y, ... 25 00
CENTRALIA.
Centralia Lodge, No. 201, by H. W. Hubbard, D. D. G. M.,...... 25 00
CHAMBERSBURG.
Chambersburg Lodge, No. 373, by C. Dennis, Sec'y,............. 25 00
CHAMPAIGN.
Western Star Lodge, No. 240, by I. H, Hess, W. M.,............ 100 00
CHARLESTON.
Charleston Lodge, No. 35, by W. E. Ginther, W. M.,............ 50 00
CHATSWORTH.
Chatsworth Lodge, No. 539, by N. C. Kenyon, Chm'n,............ 108 25
Members of Chatsworth Lodge, No. 539, by N. C. Kenyon,........ 50 00
CHEBANSE.
Chebanse Lodge, No. 429, by M. A. Swift, Sec'y,............... 62 00
CHENOA.
Chenoa Lodge, No. 292, by J. L. Colter, Sec'y,................ 30 00
CHESTER,
Chester Lodge, No. 72, by Jas. Douglass, W. M.,............... 43 00
CHESTERFIELD.
Chesterfield Lodge, No. 445, by E. C. Hall, Sec'y,............ 25 00
Members of Chesterfield Lodge, No. 445, by E. C. Hall, Sec'y,... 35 00
CHICAGO.
Members of Oriental Lodge, No. 33, by J. H. Dowland,.......... 20 00
Morris Weitzler, of Lodge, No. 33............................. 11 00
John Miller, of Hesperia Lodge, No. 411, by C. H. Brenan, W. M.. 10 00

MASONIC BOARD OF RELIEF.   71

We are indebted to the Agents of the Singer and Wheeler & Wilson Sewing Machine Co's., for discounts on Machines purchased, amounting to..$ 149 50
The total amount donated by the several Rail Roads leaving Chicago, represented by free passes and discounts on tickets purchased, is,.. 2,035 85

We are indebted for these favors, to the following named Officers, representing the Rail Road Companies, viz:
    Pennsylvania Central—W. C. Clelland, A. G. P. Agent.
    Michigan Central—Henry C. Wentworth, G. T. Agent.
    Michigan Southern—F. A. Morse, G. T. Agent.
    Chicago and Northwestern—H. P. Stanwood, G. T. Agent.
    Chicago, Rock Island & Pacific—E. St. John, G. T. Agent.
    Chicago, Burlington & Quincy—Samuel Powell, G. T. Agent.
    Illinois Central—W. P. Johnson, G. T. Agent ; W. A. Thrall, A. G. T. Agent.
    Chicago, Alton & St. Louis—James Carlton, G. T. Agent.
    Pittsburgh, Chicago & St. Louis—F. R. Myers, G. T. Agent.
    Chicago, Danville & Vincennes—C. B. Mansfield, G. T. Agent.

CLAY CITY.
Clay City Lodge, No. 488, by H. W. Hubbard, D. D. G. M.,   32 00

CLINTON.
DeWitt Lodge, No. 84, by J. Freudenstine, W. M.,................ 100 00

CLIFTON.
Craft of Clifton, by W. B. Parmeter,............................ 55 00

COURTLAND.
Courtland Lodge, No. 301, by J. Crossett, W. M.,................ 16 00

CRAWFORD.
Crawford Lodge, No. 666, by W. H. Joseph, Sec'y,................ 10 00

DALLAS CITY.
Dallas City Lodge, No. 235, by W. Scott, Sec'y,................. 25 00
Dallas City Lodge, No. 235, by W. Scott, Sec'y,................. 25 00
Dallas City Lodge, No. 235, by W. Scott, Sec'y,................. 25 00
Dallas City Lodge, No. 235, by W. Scott, Sec'y,................. 25 00

DELAVAN.
Delavan Lodge, No. 156, by T. Van Hague, W. M................... 20 00

DIXON.
Friendship Lodge, No. 7, by John D. Crabtree, W. M.,............ 100 00
Friendship Lodge, No. 7, by John D. Crabtree, W. M.,............ 28 00

DONNELSON.
Donnelson Lodge, No. 255, by H. S. Hammer, Sec'y,............... 50 00

DUDLEY.
Grandview Lodge, No. 98, by Geo. A. Gilbert, W. M., ... $ 50 00
DWIGHT.
Livingston Lodge, No. 371, by W. D. Simes, Sec'y, ... 35 50
EAST ST. LOUIS.
East St. Louis Lodge, No. 504, by L. H. Hite, ... 200 00
EARLVILLE.
Meridian Lodge, No. 183, by L. B. Paine, Sec'y, ... 50 00
EDWARDSVILLE.
Edwardsville Lodge, No. 99, by B. R. Burroughs, ... 100 00
ELIZABETH.
Kavanaugh Lodge, No. 36, by Robt. Barker, ... 55 00
ELLIOTTSVILLE.
Delia Lodge, No. 525, by H. W. Hubbard, D. D. G. M., ... 18 00
ELMWOOD.
Horeb Lodge, No. 363, by A. L. Schimpff, Sec'y, ... 20 25
EL PASO.
El Paso Lodge, No. 246, by S. T. Rogers, Treas., ... 50 00
Woodford Lodge, No. 654, by F. Cole, ... 25 00
ETNA.
Wabash Lodge, No. 179, by J. W. Montgomery, Sec'y, ... 25 00
FARMINGTON.
Farmington Lodge, No. 192, by J. Coy Kendall, W. M., ... 100 00
FAIRVIEW.
Fairview Lodge, No. 350, by S. S. Clayburg, W. M., ... 50 00
Craft of Fairview, by A. B. Morse, ... 3 00
FAIRWEATHER.
Kingston Lodge, No. 266, by M. A. Davidson, Sec'y, ... 25 00
FORREST.
Forrest Lodge, No. 614, by Lucien Bullard, W. M., ... 25 00
FORRESTON.
Forreston Lodge, No. 414, by D. H. Reynolds, ... 18 00
FOWLER.
Fowler Lodge, No. 599, by J. S. McClelland, ... 31 50
FRANKFORT.
Frankfort Lodge, No. 567, by S. D. Adams, Sec'y, ... 25 00
FRANKLIN GROVE.
Franklin Grove Lodge, No. 264, by H. N. Black, S. W., ... 32 00

MASONIC BOARD OF RELIEF. 73

FREMANTON.
Fremanton Lodge, No. 533, by H. W. Hubbard, D. D. G. M., ... $ 20 00

FREEPORT.
Excelsior Lodge, No. 97, by M. D. Chamberlain, H. C. Hackerman and W. Scott, Committee, ... 113 25
M. R. Thompson Lodge, No. 381, by L. L. Munn, D. D. G. M., .. 103 00
Evergreen Lodge, No. 170, by Wm. Young, J. P. Reed and G. P. Kingsbury, Committee, ... 130 00

FULTON CITY.
Fulton City Lodge, No. 189, by W. C. Snyder, Treas., ... 50 00

GARDNER.
Gardner Lodge, No. 573. by J. F. Benson, Sec'y, ... 50 00

GOLCONDA.
Golconda Lodge, No. 131, by J. B. Young, W. M., ... 49 75

GRAFTON.
Full Moon Lodge, No. 341, by W. S. Brinton, Sec'y, ... 20 00

GRAYVILLE.
Sheba Lodge, No. 200, by G. R. Jones, Sec'y, ... 25 00

GREENFIELD.
Greenfield Lodge, No. 129, by M. T. Nichols, Sec'y, ... 10 00

GREEN RIVER.
Clement Lodge, No. 680, by G. W. Hill, Sec'y, ... 50 00

GREENVILLE.
Greenville Lodge, No. 245, by R. L. Mudd, E. T. King and Samuel B. Hynes, Committee, 8 bbls. Flour, value.................... 52 00

GREENUP.
Greenup Lodge, No. 125, by A. J. Evarts, ... 30 00

GRIGGSVILLE.
Griggsville Lodge, No. 45, by W. H. Clark, Sec'y, ... 30 00

GROVE CITY.
Fisher Lodge, No. 585, by J. E. Harvey, Sec'y 100 00

HANOVER.
Hanover Lodge, No. 300, by A. B. White, Sec'y, ... 25 00

HARLEM.
Harlem Lodge, No. 540, by E. Cook, D. D. G. M., ... 7 00

HAVANA.

Havana Lodge, No. 88, by J. B. Paul, W. M.,	$ 100 00
Old Time Lodge, No. 629, by E. Snyder, Sec'y *pro tem.*,	25 00
Members of Old Time Lodge, No. 629, by E. Snyder, Sec'y *p. t.*,	25 00
Havana R. A. C., No. 86, by E. Snyder, Sec'y *pro tem.*,	75 00

HENNEPIN.

Social Lodge, No. 70, by C. Bodener, Sec'y,	50 00

HENRY.

Henry Lodge, No. 119, by E. T. Disonay, Sec'y,	20 00

HEYWORTH.

Heyworth Lodge, No. 251, by O. C. Rutlidge, Sec'y *pro tem.*,	50 00

HICKORY RIDGE.

Dills Lodge, No. 295, by W. Williams, Sec'y,	20 00

HIGHLAND.

Highland Lodge, No. 583, by L. E. Kinsee, Sec'y,	25 00

HILLSBORO'.

Mount Moriah Lodge, No. 51, by J. Enlow, Sec'y,	50 00

HOPEDALE.

Hopedale Lodge, No. 622, by H. M. Ford, Sec'y,	25 00

HUNTLEY GROVE.

Grafton Lodge, No. 328, by J. B. Scheimerhorn, Sec'y,	10 00

ILLIOPOLIS.

Illiopolis Lodge, No. 521, by M. H. Wilmot,	25 00

INDIANOLA.

Vermilion Lodge, No. 265, by J. K. Newkirk, Sec'y,	20 00

INDUSTRY.

Industry Lodge, No. 327, by W. H. Taylor,	25 00

IROQUOIS.

O. H. Miner Lodge, No. 506, by N. A. Biesecker, W. M.,	76 00

IRVING.

Irving Lodge, No. 455, by L. P. Deatherage, Sec'y,	16 00

JACKSONVILLE.

Jacksonville Lodge, No. 570, by S. M. Martin, W. M.,	25 00

JERSEYVILLE.

Jerseyville Lodge, No. 394, by M. R. Locke, Sec'y,	25 00
Jerseyville Lodge, No. 394, by M. R. Locke, Chm'n,	45 50

KANE.

King Solomon Lodge, No. 197, by T. Jones, Sec'y,	16 50

KANKAKEE.

Kankakee Lodge, No. 389, by John B. Dusenbury, W. M., ...$ 50 00
Craft of Kankakee, by John B. Dusenbury, W. M., ... 108 50

KINDERHOOK.

Kinderhook Lodge, No. 353, by Wm. Wilson, Treas., ... 10 00

KINGSTON MINES.

Phœnix Lodge, No. 663, by Thos. Laisley, Treas., ... 30 00

KINMUNDY.

Kinmundy Lodge, No. 398, by H. W. Hubbard, D. D. G. M., ... 25 00

LA CLEDE.

La Clede Lodge, No. 601, by H. H. Wolfe, Sec'y, ... 20 00

LA FAYETTE.

Stark Lodge, No. 501, by T. W. Ross, Sec'y, ... 25 00

LA MOILLE.

La Moille Lodge, No. 383, by Frank L. Angier, Sec'y, ... 12 00
Craft of La Moille, by F. L. Angier, ... 3 25

LANCASTER.

Lancaster Lodge, No. 106, by E. J. Jones, Com., ... 50 00

LA SALLE.

Acacia Lodge, No. 67, by Morris Friedman, Sec'y, ... 36 00

LEE CENTRE.

Lee Centre Lodge, No. 146, by R. B. Evitts, ... 25 00
Lot Chadwick, P. M. of Lodge, No. 146, by R. B. Evitts, ... 5 00

LEXINGTON.

Lexington Lodge, No. 482, by A. B. Davidson, ... 100 00

LIBERTY.

Liberty Lodge, No. 380, by J. Robbins, J. G. W., ... 50 00

LIBERTYVILLE.

Libertyville Lodge, No. 492, ... 25 00

LINCOLN.

Lincoln Lodge, No. 210, by Geo. W. Parker, W. M., ... 80 50
Logan Lodge, No. 480, by David Gillispie, ... 80 50

LITCHFIELD.

Charter Oak Lodge, No. 236, by G. M. Raymond, ... 75 00
Litchfield Lodge, No. 517, by G. M. Raymond, ... 50 00

LOCUST GROVE.

Andrew Jackson Lodge, No. 487, by M. S. Strike, ... 50 00

LOUISVILLE.

Louisville Lodge, No. 196, by S. R. Apperson,	$ 40 00
Craft of Louisville, by S. R. Apperson,	37 75

LOVINGTON.

Craft of Lovington, by W. G. Cochran, Sec'y,	35 75

MACOMB.

Craft of Macomb and Vicinity, by Wm. M. Ervin, No. 17, S. G. Wadsworth, No. 17, and S. P. Wilson, No. 553, Com.,	245 00

MAHOMET.

Mahomet Lodge, No. 220, by J. A. Brown, W. M.,	50 00

MAKANDA.

Makanda Lodge, No. 434, by F. M. Agnew, W. M.,	22 80

MALTA.

Malta Lodge, No. 320, by R. F. Lintleman, W. M.,	10 00

MALUGIN'S GROVE.

Brooklyn Lodge, No. 282, by H. H. Carnahan, W. M.,	25 00

MANITO.

Manito Lodge, No. 476, by F. Knoilhoff, W. M.,	30 00

MARENGO.

Marengo Lodge, No. 138, by J. A. Ingersol, Sec'y,	25 00

MAROA.

Maroa Lodge, No. 454, by J. A. Hood, Sec'y,	50 00

MATTOON.

Mattoon Lodge, No. 260, by E. A. Thiebens, Com.,	99 50

MELROSE.

Melrose Lodge, No. 625, by L. D. McClure,	16 25

MENDON.

Mendon Lodge, No. 449, by V. F. Kelley,	88 00

MERIDOSIA.

Benevolent Lodge, No. 52, by C. Heing, Sec'y,	25 00

METAMORA.

Metamora Lodge, No. 82, by T. L. Powers, Sec'y,	26 00

METROPOLIS.

Metropolis Lodge, No. 91, by W. J. Yost, W. H. Scott and John R. Thomas, Committee,	100 00

MILAN.
See Milan, Ohio, page 67. Twenty Dollars was received from Eureka Lodge, No. 69, located in Illinois, but owing to an error in the heading of letter covering the amount, it was credited to the Jurisdiction of Ohio.

MILBURN.
Antioch Lodge, No. 127, by D. Brewster, ...$ 10 00

MOLINE.
Doric Lodge, No. 319, by H. A. Barnard, ... 100 00
Doric Lodge, No. 319, by J. W. Morey, Com., ... 79 00

MOMENCE.
Craft of Momence, by J. L. Hamlin, H. J. Ballard and Frank R. Marcy, Committee, ... 73 50

MONMOUTH.
Trinity Lodge, No. 561, by E. C. Johnson, W. M., ... 59 00

MORRISON.
Cyrus Lodge, No. 188, by W. H. Long, W. M., ... 50 00

MOUNT AUBURN.
Kedron Lodge, No. 340, by J. H. Lawrence, H. P., ... 25 00
Kedron R. A. C., No. 138, by J. H. Lawrence, H. P., .. 25 00

MOUNT PULASKI.
Mount Pulaski Lodge, No. 87, by Geo. Meister, ... 50 00
Mount Pulaski R. A. C., No. 121, by W. P. Sawyer, ... 50 00

MOUNT STERLING.
Harden Lodge, No. 44, by A. K. Lowery, Com., ... 21 00

MOWEAQUA.
Moweaqua Lodge, No. 180, by B. Scarlitte, ... 50 00

NEOGA.
Neoga Lodge, No. 279, by Samuel F. Wilson, W. M., ... 50 00

NEW DOUGLAS.
Madison Lodge, No. 560, by W. J. Cooper, Sec'y, ... 8 00

NEW RUTLAND.
New Rutland Lodge, No. 477, by E. L. Marquis, ... 10 00

NOBLE.
Noble Lodge, No. 362, by J. T. Palmer, Com., ... 35 00

NUNDA.
Nunda Lodge, No. 169, by F. J. Wheaton, Sec'y, ... 10 00

OAKALLA.
Abraham Jonas Lodge, No. 316, by A. J. Austin, Sec'y, ... 9 00

OBLONG CITY.
Oblong City Lodge, No. 644, by A. M. Brown, Sec'y, ...$ 5 00
ODELL.
Odell Lodge, No. 401, by J. E. Williams, ... 53 00
Odell Lodge, No. 401, by J. E. Williams, ... 17 00
ODIN.
Odin Lodge, No. 503, by Thos. J. Whitehead, W. M., ... 20 00
OLNEY.
Olney Lodge, No. 140, by G. Tolle, ... 100 00
ONARGA.
Onarga Lodge, No. 305, by J. American, Sec'y, ... 24 00
OREGON.
Oregon Lodge, No. 420, by A. L. Ellinger, Treas., ... 25 00
OSKALOOSA.
Oskaloosa Lodge, No. 485, by A. Pickthall, Sec'y, ... 24 10
OTTAWA.
Occidental Lodge, No. 40, by W. S. Easton, ... 50 00
Humboldt Lodge, No. 555, by H. Mschuller, ... 25 00
OTTERVILLE.
Hamilton Lodge, No. 563, by J. T. Curtis, Treas., ... 5 00
OWANECO.
Locust Lodge, No. 623, by A. B. Leeper, W. M., ... 16 00
PALATINE.
Palatine Lodge, No. 314, by F. J. Filbert, Sec'y, ... 50 00
PALMYRA.
Palmyra Lodge, No. 463, by R. J. Allmond, Sec'y, ... 35 00
PARIS.
Prairie Lodge, No. 77, by D. G. Burr, D. D. G. M., ... 50 00
Paris Lodge, No. 268, by D. G. Burr, D. D. G. M., ... 50 00
Edgar R. A. C., No. 32, by D. G. Burr, D. D. G. M., ... 50 00
PAXTON.
Craft of Paxton, by Wilson Hoag, D. D. G. M. 120 00
PAYSON.
Payson Lodge, No. 379, by Jacob Urich, Sec'y, ... 17 00
PECATONICA.
A. W. Rawson Lodge, No. 145, by O. C. Towne, W. M., ... 100 00

MASONIC BOARD OF RELIEF. 79

PEORIA.
Temple Lodge, No. 46, by N. S. Tucker, Sec'y,	$ 200 00
Peoria Lodge, No. 15, by L. Keyon, W. M.,	161 00

PEOTONE.
Peotone Lodge, No. 636, by Chas. Gates, Sec'y,	41 50
J. B. Sollett,	5 00

PERU.
St. Johns Lodge, No. 13, by R. C. Hatenhauser,	50 00

PERRY.
Perry Lodge, No. 95, by N. D. C. Hume,	50 00
Perry Lodge, No. 95, by N. D. C. Hume,	20 00

PIPER CITY.
Piper Lodge, No. 608, by J. S. McClelland,	52 00

PLAINVIEW.
Plainview Lodge, No. 461, by John Tunnell, W. M.,	14 90

PLEASANT HILL.
S. R. Connor & Co., 12 bbls. Flour, value,	78 00

PLYMOUTH.
Plymouth Lodge, No. 286, by J. Robbins, J. G. W.,	10 00

POCAHONTAS.
Gordon Lodge, No. 473, by W. V. Wiese, Treas.,	25 00

PONTOOSUC.
Herrick Lodge, No. 193, by L. H. Harper, Sec'y,	25 00

POTOSI.
Bethseda Lodge, No. 661, by A. W. Green, Sec'y,	19 00

PRAIRIE CITY.
Golden Gate Lodge, No. 248, by T. L. Magee, W. M.,	16 00
Golden Gate Lodge, No. 248, by T. L. Magee, W. M.,	2 50
Golden Gate Lodge, No. 248, by T. L. Magee, W. M., 4 boxes Clothing, estimated value,	200 00

QUINCY.
Craft of Quincy, by William Harvey, W. M.,	1,000 00
Craft of Quincy, by J. Robbins, J. G. W.,	22 00
Craft of Quincy, by J. Robbins, J. G. W.,	11 00
Craft of Quincy, by J. Robbins, J. G. W.,	4 00

RANTOUL.
Rantoul Lodge, No. 470, by J. W. Dodge, W. M.,	57 25

ROCKFORD.
Craft of Rockford, by Seely Perry, Committee,	600 00

ROCK ISLAND.
Craft of Rock Island, by V. M. Blanding, ... 50 75
Trio Lodge, No. 57, by W. L. Sweeney, Sec'y, ... 100 00
Trio Lodge, No. 57, by W. L. Sweeney, Sec'y, ... 50 00
RUSHVILLE.
Rushville Lodge, No. 9, by J. C. Bagby, W. M., ... 58 00
SADORUS.
J. R. Gorin Lodge, No. 537, by S. H. Smith, Sec'y, ... 34 00
SANDWICH.
Meteor Lodge, No. 283, by Committee, ... 100 00
SAN JOSE.
San Jose Lodge, No. 645, by E. Rogers, W. M., ... 12 25
SAVANNA.
Mississippi Lodge, No. 385, by A. H. Hershey, W. M., ... 10 50
SHAWNEETOWN.
Warren Lodge, No. 14, by F. L. Rhodes, ... 25 00
SHELDON.
Sheldon Lodge, No. 609, by L. B. Brown, Treas., ... 88 50
SHIPMAN.
Shipman Lodge, No. 212, by W. G. Wallace, ... 15 00
SPARLAND.
Sparland Lodge, No. 441, by T. E. Gasper and J. V. Mills, Com., 48 00
SPARTA.
Hope Lodge, No. 162, by W. P. Askin, Sec'y, ... 25 00
SPRINGFIELD.
R. W. Orlin H. Miner, Grand Secretary, of the Grand Lodge, of the State of Illinois, ... 100 00
STERLING.
Craft of Sterling, by M. S. Bowman, of No. 612, ... 57 00
Craft of Sterling, by M. S. Bowman, W. M., ... 1 50
STONE FORT.
Stone Fort Lodge, No. 495, by W. R. Mizell, P. M., ... 6 00
STONE'S PRAIRIE.
Adams Lodge, No. 529, by J. Robbins, J. G. W., ... 13 00
SUMMERFIELD.
Summerfield Lodge, No. 342, by J. H. Hewett, W. M., ... 14 85
SYCAMORE.
Sycamore Lodge, No. 134, by D. Dustin, ... 73 59

TENNESSEE.
Tennessee Lodge, No. 496, by H. L. Rapelye, -------------- $ 10 00
TIME.
Time Lodge, No. 569, by E. F. Binns, W. M., ----------------- 10 00
TISKILWA.
Sharon Lodge, No. 550, by John H. Welch, ------------------- 25 00
TOLONO.
Tolono Lodge, No. 391, by A. T. Darrah, W. M., -------------- 40 00
Tolono Lodge, No. 391, by A. T. Darrah, W. M., -------------- 15 50
TOULON.
Toulon Lodge, No. 93, by C. Meyers, Sec'y, ------------------ 10 00
Toulon Lodge, No. 93, by C. Meyers, Sec'y, ------------------ 20 00
TOWANDA.
Towanda Lodge, No. 542, ----------------------------------- 25 00
TRENTON.
Trenton Lodge, No. 109, by J. Wahrenberger, Sec'y, ----------- 79 50
TROY GROVE.
Shiloh Lodge, No. 397, by H. Wienhard, --------------------- 10 00
TUSCOLA.
Centre Star Lodge, No. 651, by J. A. Franks, ---------------- 20 00
VANDALIA.
Temperance Lodge, No. 16, by H. W. Hubbard, D. D. G. M., ---- 50 00
VENICE.
Venice Lodge, No. 621, by S. W. Huddleston, S. W., ---------- 20 35
VERMILION.
Stratton Lodge, No. 408, by B. F. Table, Sec'y, -------------- 25 00
Stratton Lodge, No. 408, by J. Wrings, Treas., -------------- 25 00
VIENNA.
Vienna Lodge, No. 150, by J. T. Smith, Sec'y, --------------- 25 00
VIOLA.
Viola Lodge, No. 577, by B. Milliken, W. M., ---------------- 21 00
VIRDEN.
Virden Lodge, No. 161, by L. A. Virden, W. M., -------------- 100 00
Brethren of Virden Lodge, No. 161, by L. A. Virden, W. M., --- 20 00
VIRGINIA.
Virginia Lodge, No. 544, by G. F. Hillig, W. M., ------------- 50 35
WALNUT GROVE.
Altona Lodge, No. 330, by J. S. Chambers, ------------------ 22 00

WALSHVILLE.
Walshville Lodge, No. 475, by T. C. Kirtland, W. M., ... $ 43 50
WATSEKA.
Watseka Lodge, No. 446, by J. L. Donovan and Wm. Conley, Com., 165 00
WARREN.
Jo Daviess Lodge, No. 278, by S. A. Clark, Sec'y, ... 50 00
WAUKEGAN.
Waukegan Lodge, No. 78, by A. T. Blodgett, W. M., ... 100 00
One box, four bbls. and one bag, containing Clothing, Provisions and Vegetables—donor unknown—estimated value, ... 60 00
WAVERLY.
Waverly Lodge, No. 118, by H. Watson, Sec'y, ... 10 00
WHITE ROCK.
Meridian Sun Lodge, No. 505, by E. P. Allen, ... 50 00
WILLIAMSBURG.
Cold Spring Lodge, No. 513, by Thos. Fritz, Sec'y, ... 10 00
WILMINGTON.
Wilmington Lodge, No. 208, by E. B. Fisher, Sec'y, ... 70 50
WINDSOR.
Windsor Lodge, No. 322, by Jas. I. Templeton, Sec'y, ... 50 00
WYANETT.
Wyanett Lodge, No. 231, by J. H. Cass, ... 50 00
WYOMING.
Wyoming Lodge, No. 479, by J. W. Agard, Gr. Chaplain, ... 20 00
Wyoming Chapter, No. 53, O. E. S., by J. W. Agard, Gr. Chaplain, One box Clothing; material cost $30, value when made into garments, ... 67 50
YOUNGSTOWN.
Youngstown Lodge, No. 387, by A. A. Hoesington, ... 25 00

Goods received from unknown points and parties, value, ... 300 50

Total amount received from Illinois, ... $15,897 85

STATE OF KENTUCKY.

LOUISVILLE.

In order to make a full exhibit of the contributions received by this Board from the Fraternity at Louisville, we publish a part of the report of the Committee of Masonic Relief, of Louisville, organized for the relief of the sufferers by the Chicago Fire, showing their receipts, viz :

MASONIC BOARD OF RELIEF. 83

M. W. Grand Lodge of Kentucky, -------------- $1,000 00
Bro. C. Henry Finck, ----------------------------- 250 00
Bro. Geo. W. Wicks, ----------------------------- 250 00
Bro. Evard Jewell, ------------------------------ 87 50
Hiram Lodge, No. 4, Frankfort, ------------------- 179 50
Lexington R. A. C., No. 1, Lexington, ------------ 50 00
Craft of Somerset, by Bro. L. B. Porch, ---------- 43 00
Craft of Louisville, ---------------------------- 1,731 17
Craft of Louisville, in Goods donated, value, ---- 135 55
                         ———— $3,726 72

Of this amount we received, in Cash, ------------ 1,588 75
And in Dry Goods, Clothing, etc., purchased by request of
 the President of this Board, -------------- 2,137 97
                       $3,726 72

We received from the LOUISVILLE GENERAL RELIEF COMMITTEE,
 located at Chicago, per Brethren Garrabrant, Hazlitt,
 McClellan, Franks, Crane and Reed, Dry Goods, Cook-
 ing Stoves and Provisions, to the value of ------- 1,597 75
One box Clothing, from a Brother of Excelsior Lodge, No. 258, .. 5 00

NEWPORT.
Craft of Newport and Friends of Masonry, by J. J. Raipe, Com., .. 400 00

Total amount received from Kentucky, --------------- $5,729 47

In justice to our Brethern of Kentucky, it should be stated that they generously tendered to the homeless widows and children of Chicago, the hospitalities of their noble Institution, *The Masonic Widows' and Orphans' Home*, located at Louisville.

STATE OF MICHIGAN.
BATH.
One box Boots and Shoes, from H. P. Stewart, ---------------- $26 25

Total amount received from Michigan, ------------------ $26 25

STATE OF MINNESOTA.
PRESTON.
Preston Lodge, No. 36, by Abram Kalder, W. M., -------------- $ 25 00
ST. PETER.
Nicollet Lodge, No. 54, by Wm. Combs, Gr. Sec'y, ------------ 50 00

Total amount received from Minnesota, ----------------- $75 00

STATE OF IOWA.

BELLE PLAINE.
Mount Horeb R. A. C., No. 45, by E. A. Guilbert, G. H. P., ...$ 25 00

BLOOMFIELD.
Bloomfield R. A. C., No. 25, by E. A. Guilbert, G. H. P., ... 25 00

BOONSBORO'.
Tuscan R. A. C., No. 31, by E. A. Guilbert, G. H. P.,............ 10 00

CEDAR FALLS.
Valley R. A. C., No. 20, by E. A. Guilbert, G. H. P., ... 5 00

CEDAR RAPIDS.
Crescent Lodge, No. 25, by S. Neidig, Sec'y, ... 10 00

CHARLES CITY.
St. Charles Lodge, No. 141, by C. Ditmore, ... 6 25
Almond R. A. C., No. 53, by H. C. Raymond, ... 6 25

CLARINDA.
Clarinda R. A. C., No. 29, by E. A. Guilbert, G. H. P., ... 10 00

COUNCIL BLUFFS.
Craft of Council Bluffs, by Geo. W. Lininger, E. C., ... 500 00

This donation was sent by the Sir Knights of Ivanhoe Commandery, No. 17, and the Fraternity at Council Bluffs. The money had been collected to entertain the Grand Commandery and Grand Chapter of Iowa, which was soon to meet at Council Bluffs. The following extract from a letter will explain:

COUNCIL BLUFFS, IOWA, Oct. 10th, 1871.
D. C. CREGIER, Grand Master A. F. &. A. Masons:

Dear Brother:—Our Grand Commandery and Chapter are to meet next week. We have raised five or six hundred dollars towards a banquet for them. That money is now yours. We cannot think of banqueting whilst our Brethren in Chicago are suffering. * * * To be distributed as you think best. * * *   Fraternally Yours,
GEORGE W. LININGER, E. C.

CRESCO.
Shiloh R. A. C., U. D., by E. A. Guilbert, G. H. P., ...$ 5 00

DAVENPORT.
Davenport Lodge, No. 37, by C. S. Streeper, W. M.,............... 162 00
Trinity Lodge, No. 208, by D. N. Richardson, W. M.,.............. 20 00
Fraternal Lodge, No. 221, by F. W. Angle, W. M.,................. 70 00

DECORAH.
Great Lights Lodge, No. 181, by T. A. Watson, W. M. 200 00

DES MOINES.

Pioneer Lodge, No. 22, by W. A. Colton, W. M.,	$ 150 00
Capital Lodge, No. 110, by Jos. M. Griffiths, W. M.,	200 00

DUBUQUE.

Siloam Commandery, No. 3, by E. A. Guilbert, G. H. P.,	15 00

FORT DODGE.

Delta R. A. C., No. 51, by E. A. Guilbert, G. H. P.,	10 00

INDEPENDENCE.

Aholiab R. A. C., No. 21, by E. A. Guilbert, G. H. P.,	25 00

IOWA CITY.

Iowa City R. A. C., No. 2, by H. S. Bixby, Sec'y,	10 00

LANSING.

Mark Well R. A. C., No. 30, by H. H. Hemmingway, H. P.,	10 00

MARSHALLTOWN.

Signet R. A. C., No. 38, by A. C. Abbott, H. P.,	100 00

MONTICELLO.

Monticello R. A. C., No. 42, by E. A. Guilbert, G, H. P.,	5 00

MOUNT PLEASANT.

Henry R. A. C., No. 8, by E. A. Guilbert, G. H. P.,	10 00

MUSCATINE.

Washington R. A. C., No. 54, by E. A. Guilbert, G. H. P.,	5 00

NEW JEFFERSON.

Corner Stone R. A. C., No. 64, by E. A. Guilbert, G. H. P.,	5 00

NEWTON.

Grebal R. A. C., No. 12, by E. A. Guilbert, G. H. P.,	25 00

OTTUMWA.

Clinton R. A. C., No. 9, by E. A. Guilbert, G. H. P.,	20 00

OSKALOOSA.

Hiram R. A. C., No. 6, by E. A. Guilbert, G. H. P.,	5 00

RED OAK JUNCTION.

Montgomery R. A. C., No. 57, by E. A. Guilbert, G. H. P.,	5 00

SIDNEY.

Shekinah R. A. C., No. 44, by E. A. Guilbert, G. H. P.,	10 00

SIOUX CITY.

Sioux City R. A. C., No. 26, by E. A. Guilbert, G. H. P.,	5 00

TIPTON.

Siloam R. A. C., No. 19, by E. A. Guilbert, G. H. P.,	10 00

VINTON.
Adoniram R. A. C., No. 15, by E. A. Guilbert, G. H. P., ... $ 10 00
WATERLOO.
Tabernacle R. A. C., No. 52, by E. A. Guilbert, G. H. P., ... 10 00

Total amount received from Iowa, ... $1,699 50

It is deemed proper to state that Bro. E. A. Guilbert also received donations from Dubuque R. A. C., No. 3, Dubuque, $10 ; Keystone R. A. C., No. 32, Clinton, $5 ; and Marion R. A. C., No. 10, Marion, $5 ; but having received notice from the President of this Board, that further aid was not needed, Bro. Guilbert returned the amounts above named to the donors.

Bro. T. Schriener, Grand Tyler of Iowa, collected and forwarded One Hundred and Fifty Dollars to the President of this Board, with the request that he present the amount to W. Bro. John P. Ferns, Grand Tyler of Illinois, in behalf of the Tylers of Iowa, which was done in accordance with above instructions.

STATE OF MISSOURI.

M. W. Grand Lodge of Missouri, by Geo. Frank Gouley, G. S., $1,000 00
SAINT JOSEPH.
St. Joseph Lodge, No. 78, by J. S. Brown, P. M., ... 225 00
Zeredatha Lodge, No. 189, by D. M. McDonald, Sec'y, ... 50 00
SAINT LOUIS.
Occidental Lodge, No. 163, by D. J. Mange, Sec'y, ... 175 00

Total amount received from Missouri, ... $1,450 00

STATE OF KANSAS.

M. W. Grand Lodge of Kansas, by J. M. Price, G. M., ... $500 00
EASTON.
Easton Lodge, No. 45, by J. M. Price, G. M., ... 10 00
HIAWATHA.
Hiawatha Lodge, No. 35, by J. M. Price, G. M., ... 10 00
LAWRENCE.
Lawrence Lodge, No. 6, by J. M. Price, G. M., ... 78 00
LEAVENWORTH.
Leavenworth Lodge, No. 2, by J. M. Price, G. M., ... 120 00
MOUNT PLEASANT.
Mount Pleasant Lodge, No. 58, by J. M. Price, G. M., ... 10 00

OSAGE MISSION.

Mission Lodge, No. 92, by J. M. Price, G. M., ------------------- $ 9 00

TROY.

Troy Lodge, No. 55, by J. M. Price, G. M., ------------------- 22 50

Total amount received from Kansas, ------------------- $759 50

STATE OF NEBRASKA.

FREMONT.

Fremont Lodge, No. 15, by W. H. Munger, Sec'y, --------------- $ 21 90

OMAHA:

Capital Lodge, No. 3, by M. Dunham, D. D. G. M., --------------- 200 00
Capital Lodge, No. 3, by M. Dunham, D. D. G. M., --------------- 255 00

O'FALLON'S STATION.

James Egan, Capt. 2nd Cavalry, U. S. A., by H. P. Deuel, P. G. M. 204 00

Total amount received from Nebraska, ------------------- $680 90

STATE OF NEVADA.

CARSON CITY.

Carson Lodge No. 1, by J. J. Linn, ------------------- $300 00
Add premium on gold, ------------------- 33 00—333 00

VIRGINIA CITY.

Virginia Lodge No. 3, by J. C. Currie, W. M., ---------- 200 00
Add premium on gold, ------------------------- 22 00—222 00

Total amount received from Nevada, ------------------- $555 00

STATE OF CALIFORNIA.

[Extract from the Proceedings of the Grand Lodge of California.]

MORNING SESSION, Oct. 11th, 1871.

Resolved, That Five Thousand Dollars, in coin, of the funds of this Grand Lodge, now in the hands of the Trustees of the Reserve Fund, be donated and immediately forwarded to the Grand Master of Masons in Illinois, in aid of the sufferers by the late conflagration in Chicago. * * * * And it was unanimously adopted by the Grand Lodge.

Resolved, That, as a further evidence of our practical sympathy, the box of Masonic Charity be placed upon the altar, at 2 o'clock this afternoon, and that the Brethren be requested to cast their offerings therein, as God has blessed and favored them; and that the money thus contributed be also transmitted by our Grand Master, without delay, to the Grand Master of Illinois, to be disbursed according to his own judgment, for the relief of destitute Masons and their families. Which resolution was adopted.

AFTERNOON SESSION, Oct. 11th, 1871.

This being the hour appointed at the morning session, the contribution box was placed upon the altar, and the sum of One Thousand and Five Dollars, in coin, was found to have been contributed by members of the Grand Lodge, as a further donation to the sufferers by the disaster in Chicago.

M. W. GRAND LODGE OF CALIFORNIA, by L. E. Pratt, G. M.....$6,800 00

ALLEGHANY.
Forest Lodge, No. 66, by A. G. Abell, Gr. Sec'y,................... 55 50

MILLVILLE.
Northern Light Lodge, No. 190, by A. G. Abell, Gr. Sec'y, ... 48 35

SACRAMENTO.
Craft employed by the Central Pacific Railroad, of California, by Bro. A. Egl,............................. 39 00
Add premium on gold,............................. 3 90 —42 90

SAN FRANCISCO.
Golden Gate Lodge, No. 30, by Henry Blythe, W. M.,..... 222 10
Add premium on gold,............................. 24 43—246 53

SMARTSVILLE.
Rose Bar Lodge, No. 89, by A. G. Abell, Gr. Sec'y,............... 112 00

STOCKTON.
Fred. E. Lux, ... 30 00
Morning Star Lodge, No. 68, by J. S. Greenwood, E. Block and L. E. Lyon, Com.,......................... 150 00
Add premium on gold,............................. 16 50—166 50

Total amount received from California,...............$7,501 78

STATE OF OREGON.
BAKER CITY.
Baker Lodge, No. 47, by J. W. Wisdom, Sec'y,.................. $100 00

Total amount received from Oregon, ... $100 00

COLORADO TERRITORY.
GEORGETOWN.
Washington Lodge, No. 12, by J. A. Burdick, W. M., ... $42 00

Total amount received from Colorado, ... $42 00

MASONIC BOARD OF RELIEF. 89

IDAHO TERRITORY.
IDAHO CITY.
Idaho R. A. C., by J. W. Brown, Sec'y, ---------------$100 00
Add premium on gold,------------------------- 11 00—111 00

Total amount received from Idaho Territory,-------------$111 00

DACOTAH TERRITORY.
YANKTON.
St. John's Lodge, No. 166, by L. M. Purdy, ---- --------------..... $60 50

Total amount received from Dacotah Territory,------------ $60 50

UTAH TERRITORY.
SALT LAKE CITY.
Craft of Salt Lake City, by A. S. Gould, -----------------------$230 00

Total amount received from Utah Territory,---------------$230 00

NEW MEXICO.
ELIZABETHTOWN.
Kit Carson Lodge, No. 326, by G. Frank Gouley, Gr. Sec'y of Mo., $100 00

Total amount received from New Mexico,------------------$100 00

FOREIGN DONATIONS.

DOMINION OF CANADA.
(Jurisdiction of the Grand Lodge of A. F. & A. Masons of Canada.)

M. W. Grand Lodge of Canada, by James Seymour,
  G. M.,---------------------------------$2,000 00
  Add premium on gold,----------------------- 216 78—2,216 78

KINGSTON.
W. G. Bartell, -------/------------------ -------------------- 4 00

TORONTO.
St. Andrew's Lodge, No. 16, by A. N. Boswell, Gr. Sec'y,. 100 00
  Add premium on gold,----------------------- 11 00–111 00
King Solomon's Lodge, No. 22, by A. N. Boswell, Gr. Sec'y, 100 00
  Add premium on gold,----------------------- 11 00—111 00
Ionic Lodge, No. 25, by A. N. Boswell, Gr. Sec'y,-------- 100 00
  Add premium on gold,----------------------- 11 00—111 00

Rehoboam Lodge, No. 65, by A. N. Boswell, Gr. Sec'y, ..$ 100 00
    Add premium on gold,........................... 11 00—111 00
St. John's Lodge, No. 75, by A. N. Boswell, Gr. Sec'y,... 100 00
    Add premium on gold,........................... 11 00—111 00
Wilson Lodge, No. 86, by A. N. Boswell, Gr. Sec'y,...... 100 00
    Add premium on gold,........................... 11 00—111 00
Stephenson Lodge, No. 218, by A. N. Boswell, Gr. Sec'y, 100 00
    Add premium on gold,........................... 11 00—111 00

WELLINGTON DISTRICT.

Craft of Wellington District, by A. B. Petrie, D. D. G. M., 754 00
    Add premium on gold,........................... 82 94—836 94

Contributed by Speed   Lodge, No. 180, and Masons of Guelph, Ont.
    Alma   "   " 72,   "   Galt,   "
    Irvine   "   " 203,   "   Elora,   "
    St. Albans "   " 200.   "   Mt. Forest, "
    New Dominion " 205,   "   New Hamburg,
    Harris   " 216,   "   Orangeville.

WILSON DISTRICT.

Craft of Wilson District, by P. J. Brown, D. D. G. M.,............ 143 75

Total amount from above Jurisdiction, ----------------$3,978 47

(Jurisdiction of the Grand Lodge of Quebec, A. F. & A. M.)

DUNHAM.
Prevost Lodge, No. 2, by John H. Isaacson, Gr. Sec'y,.... 40 00
    Add premium on gold,........................... 5 57— 45 57

FRELIGSBURG.
Freligsburg Lodge, No. 22, by John H. Isaacson, Gr. Sec'y, 30 00
    Add premium on gold,........................... 4 18— 34 18

LACOLE.
Hoyle Lodge, No. 9, by John H. Isaacson, Gr. Sec'y,.... 20 00
    Add premium on gold,........................... 2 78— 22 78

MONTREAL.
St. George Lodge, No. 6, by John H. Graham, G. M.,.... 100 00
    Add premium on gold,........................... 11 00—111 00
Zetland Lodge, No. 7, by Jno. H. Graham, G. M., ... 100 00
    Add premium on gold,........................... 11 00—111 00
Kilwinning Lodge, No. 13, by John H. Graham, G. M.,.. 150 00
    Add premium on gold,........................... 16 50—166 50
Victoria Lodge, No. 17, by John H. Isaacson, Gr. Sec'y,.. 50 00
    Add premium on gold,........................... 6 97— 56 97

QUEBEC CITY.

Albion Lodge, No. 0, by John H. Graham, G. M., ... $ 50 00
   Add premium on gold, ... 5 50— 55 50
St. Andrew Lodge, No. 5, by John H. Isaacson, Gr. Sec'y, 50 00
   Add premium on gold, ... 6 96— 56 96

ST. ARMAND STATION.

Nelson Lodge, No. 3, by John H. Isaacson, Gr. Sec'y, ... 10 00
   Add premium on gold,.............................. 1 40— 11 40

Total amount from above Jurisdiction, ... $671 86

NEW FOUNDLAND.
ST. JOHNS.

Tasker Lodge, No. 454, by C. A. & R. Society, ... $ 220 50
St. John's Lodge, No. 559, by C. S. Pincent, ... 80 00
   Add premium on gold, ... 10 89— 90 89
Avalin Lodge, No. 776, by G. A. Hutchins, W. M., ... 144 60
   Add premium on gold, ... 15 90—160 50

Total amount received from New Foundland, ... $471 89

Total amount received from the Dominion of Canada. $5,122 22

CENTRAL AMERICA.
ISTHMUS OF PANAMA.

Manzanillo Lodge, No. 25, and sojourning Brethern, per M. W.
   Jno. H. Anthon, of N. Y., ... $259 85
Isthmus Lodge, No. 98, by M. W. J. W. Simonds, N. Y., ... 325 00

Total amount received from Central America, ... $584 85

ENGLAND.
DERBYSHIRE.

Craft of Derbyshire, by William Naylor, P. G. Sec'y, £74, 2s.,
   6d., value, ... $394 63

Total amount received from England, ... $394 63

BRITISH INDIA.
BOMBAY.

Master of Cyrus Lodge, Bombay, by B. F. Farnum, U. S. Consul
   at Jubblepore, 50 Rupees, value, ... $26 65

Total amount received from British India, ... $26 65

RECAPITULATION.

Maine,	$ 450 00
New Hampshire,	200 00
Massachusetts,	7,402 71
Rhode Island,	100 00
Connecticut,	2,387 12
New York,	18,636 28
New Jersey,	4,441 20
Pennsylvania,	9,607 15
Maryland,	86 50
Virginia,	117 00
District of Columbia,	3,022 30
South Carolina,	25 00
Louisiana,	400 00
Ohio,	699 00
Indiana,	1,069 00
Illinois,	15,897 85
Kentucky,	5,729 47
Michigan,	26 25
Minnesota,	75 00
Iowa,	1,699 50
Missouri,	1,450 00
Kansas,	759 50
Nebraska,	680 90
Nevada,	555 00
California,	7,501 78
Oregon,	100 00
Colorado Territory	42 00
Idaho Territory,	111 00
Dacotah Territory,	60 50
Utah Territory,	230 00
New Mexico,	100 00
Dominion of Canada,	5,122 22
Central America,	584 85
England,	394 63
British India,	26 65
Interest on Deposits in Bank,	844 14

Total amount received from all sources, ... $90,634 50
    "   "   Cash received, ... $82,244 92
    "   "   Interest on deposits, ... 844 14
    "   "   Merchandise received, ... 7,545 44

                                                   $90,634 50

MASONIC BOARD OF RELIEF. 93

ACCOUNT OF THE DISBURSEMENTS.

Date.	To whom paid, and on what account.	No.	Voucher.	Amt.
Oct. 16	—A Brother, app. No. 1,	A	1,	$ 5 00
	do app. No. 182,	A	2,	8 00
21	—Geo. R. McClellan, for relief of app. No. 19,	A	3,	10 00
23	—C. J. Franks, for relief of app. Nos. 16 and 20,	A	4,	16 00
24	—A Brother, app. No. 25,	A	5,	50 00
	do app. No. 159,	A	6,	50 00
				$139 00

[NOTE.—The above is an account of the money drawn from the Treasury and disbursed by order of the Board. GEO. K. HAZLITT, Sec'y.]

Oct. 24	—Dr. Powell, for relief of app. No. 42,	B	1,	$100 00
	A Brother, app. No. 153,	B	2,	10 00
	do app. No. 6,	B	3,	2 75
	do app. No. 13,	B	4,	5 00
	do app. No. 18,	B	5,	20 00
	do app. No. 362,	B	6,	5 00
	do app. No. 8,	B	7,	6 00
	do app. No. 205,	B	8,	12 00
	do app. No. 226,	B	9,	8 00
	do app. No. 14,	B	10,	5 00
	do app. No. 17,	B	11,	3 00
	C. J. Franks, for Relief of app. No. 259,	B	12,	8 00
	do " app. No. 12,	B	13,	6 00
	A Brother, app. No. 44,	B	14,	5 00
	do app. No. 240,	B	15,	8 00
	E. J. Hill, Expense acc't, Stationery, &c.,	B	16.	25 00
	A Brother, app. No. 3,	B	17,	3 00
	do app. No. 96,	B	18,	7 00
	do app. No. 9,	B	19,	10 00
	Geo. R. McClellan, R. R. Tickets for applicants,	B	20,	15 75
	M. M's. Widow, app. No. 299,	B	21,	25 00

FINAL REPORT OF THE

Date.	To whom paid, and on what account.	No. Voucher.	Amt.
Oct. 24.—	J. Morison, for Relief of a Sick Brother,	B 22,	$ 4 45
	C. H. Brenan, " do	B 23,	39 43
	A Brother, app. No. 263,	B 24,	19 58
	M. M's. Widow, app. No. 82,	B 25,	5 00
	A Brother, app. No. 240,	B 26,	7 00
	do app. No. —,	B 27,	5 00
	E. J. Hill, Expense acc't, Incidental,	B 28,	7 00
			$376 96

[NOTE.—The above is the account of the disbursement of money by Bro. E. J. HILL, Acting Superintendent, Oct. 24th, 1871.]

Here begins the Cash account of the Board from Oct. 25th, the date of the permanent organization.

Oct. 25—	M. M's. Widow, app. No. 97,	1,	$ 5 00
	A Brother, app. No. 98,	2,	11 00
	Western News Co., Expense acc't, Stationery,	3,	2 90
	Norton & Co., Mdse., Flour,	4,	66 50
	I. W. Congdon, for Relief of app. No. 44,	5,	5 65
	J. Morison, Expense acc't, advertising,	6,	12 50
	M. M's. Widow, app. No. 93,	7,	5 00
26—	H. F. Holcomb, for Relief of app. No. 63,	8,	3 00
	C. H. Brenan, Labor acc't, services,	9,	50 00
	H. F. Holcomb, Labor acc't, services,	10,	25 00
	A Brother, app. No. 104,	11,	15 00
	M. M's Widow, app. No. 108,	12,	10 00
	E. J. Hill, for Relief of app. No. 21,	13,	9 70
	C. H. Brenan, " app. No. 75,	14,	3 00
	A Brother, app. No. 94,	15,	45 00
	W. H. Davenport, for Relief of app, No. 52,	16,	2 00
27—	E. Ronayne, " app. No. 151,	17,	2 00
	Culver, Page & Hoyne, Expense acc't, Stationery,	18,	2 60
28—	A Brother, app. No. 92,	19,	5 00
	Geo. W. Scott, for app. No. 177,	20,	27 00
	J. Morison, Mdse., Stove,	21,	5 00
	A Brother, app. No. 179,	22,	16 00
	F. A. Feder, for Relief of app. No. 211,	23,	3 00
30—	J. W. Sterns & Sons, Mdse., Groceries,	24,	60 25
	J. McLarren, for Relief of app. No. 225,	25,	4 00
	I. W. Congdon, Expense acc't, Twine,	26,	1 00
	Norton & Co., Mdse., Flour,	27,	66 50
31—	G. R. McClellan, for Relief of app. No. 240,	28,	6 00
	do " app. No. 237,	29,	1 00

MASONIC BOARD OF RELIEF. 95

Date,	To whom paid, and on what account.	No. Voucher.	Amt.
Oct. 31.—	T. H. Agnew, Expense acc't, Locks, Keys, &c.,	30,	$ 3 00
	R. H. Mason, Mdse., Stoves,	31,	382 00
	C. H. Brenan, for Relief of app. No. 195,	32,	9 50
	Noble & Little, " app. No. 189,	33,	5 00
	A. Weise, " app. No. 256,	34,	50 00
	H. F. Holcomb, " app. No. 135,	35,	25 00
Nov. 1—	J. Morison, Supt., Mdse., cash expended for supplies,	36,	27 60
	Field, Leiter & Co., Mdse., Dry Goods,	37,	475 00
	C. Johnstone, for Relief of app. No. 85,	38,	25 00
	H. F. Holcomb, " app. No. 237,	39,	5 00
	Richards & Gooch, Mdse., Groceries,	40,	427 65
	Geo. B. Carpenter, for Relief of app. No. 285.	41,	25 00
	do " app. No. 286,	42,	25 00
	do " app. No. 287,	43,	25 00
2—	C. H. Brenan. " app. No. 280,	44,	20 00
	E. J. Hill, " app. No. 290,	45,	20 00
	Norton & Co., Mdse., Flour,	46,	65 00
	G. S. Richardson, Mdse., Boots and Shoes,	47,	123 00
	E. J. Hill, for Relief of app. No. 299,	48,	15 00
	J. E. Pettibone, Labor acc't, Teaming,	49,	12 00
	A. H. Small, Labor acc't, services,	50,	12 00
	John P. Ferns, " "	51,	8 00
	W. H. Davenport, " "	52,	18 00
	J. Morison, " "	53,	23 10
	H. Duvall, " "	54,	23 10
3—	Culver, Page & Hoyne, Expense, Stationery,	55,	8 15
	I. W. Congdon, for Relief of app. No. 97,	56,	4 75
	E. J. Hill, Mdse., Stove,	57,	15 00
4—	A. H. Small, Labor acc't,	58,	24 00
	E. J. Hill, for Relief of app. No. 311.	59,	16 15
	D. C. Cregier, " app. No. 59,	60,	7 50
6—	Field, Leiter & Co., Mdse.. Dry Goods,	61,	445 13
	John Sutton, for Relief of app. No. 253,	62,	25 00
	D. C. Cregier, " app. No. 155,	63,	48 50
	G. S. Richardson & Co., Mdse., Boots and Shoes	64,	117 00
7—	J. V. Farwell & Co., Mdse., Dry Goods,	65,	309 30
	J. W. Stearns & Sons, Mdse., Groceries,	66,	63 58
8—	Hartwell Bros., Mdse., Coal,	67,	256 90
	E. Ronayne, for Relief of app. No. 352,	68,	5 25
	C. C. Mnfg. Co., Mdse., Cutlery,	69,	27 18
10—	R. H. Mason, Mdse., Stoves,	70,	501 00
	I. W. Congdon, for relief of app. No. 355,	71,	20 00
	Bonsfield & Poole, Mdse., Wooden Ware,	72,	51 58
13—	Field, Leiter & Co., Mdse., Dry Goods,	73,	46 26

Date.	To whom paid, and on what account.	No. Voucher.	Amt.
Nov. 13.—	J. V. Farwell & Co., Mdse., Dry Goods,	74,	$ 48 96
14—	A. Schmidt, for Relief of app. No. 237,	75,	35 00
	Norton & Co., Mdse., Flour,	76,	65 00
	Reno & Little, Mdse., Fuel,	77,	240 50
	C. Robinson, for relief of app. No. 314,	78,	50 00
15—	G. S. Richardson & Co., Mdse., Boots and Shoes,	79,	72 00
	Clement, Morton & Co., Mdse., Clothing,	80,	244 50
	Field, Leiter & Co., Mdse., Dry Goods,	81,	164 10
	J. Morison, Supt., Mdse., Cash expended for supplies,	82,	102 69
17—	Reno & Little, for relief of app. No. 353,	83,	9 00
	J. W. Stearns & Sons, Mdse., Groceries,	84,	48 00
18—	B. C. Jones, Mdse., Hardware,	85,	59 90
	Colby & Werts, Mdse., Furniture,	86,	183 68
	C. J. Franks, for relief of app. No. 394,	87,	25 00
	W. W. Strong, Mdse., Furniture,	88,	130 05
	Richards & Gooch, Mdse., Groceries,	89,	128 33
20—	J. Morison, Supt., Mdse., Cash expended for supplies,	90,	30 25
	G. S. Richardson & Co., Mdse., Boots and Shoes,	91,	80 50
	R. H. Mason, Mdse., Stoves,	92,	343 00
	Wm. Gough, for relief of app. No. 153,	93,	8 00
23—	C. J. Franks, for relief of app. No. 112,	94,	8 00
	Tillotson Bros., Mdse., Stoves,	95,	343 75
	W. M. Egan, Treas., for a protested draft returned,	96,	51 56
24—	J. W. Stearns & Sons, Mdse., Groceries,	97,	78 04
	Richards & Gooch, Mdse., Groceries,	98,	41 50
	J. Morison, Supt., Mdse., Cash expended for supplies,	99,	112 20
25—	J. V. Farwell & Co., Mdse., Dry Goods,	100,	118 40
	D. H. Kilmore, for relief of app. No. 419,	101,	22 00
	W. W. Strong, Mdse., Furniture,	102,	107 25
27—	G. S. Richardson & Co., Mdse., Boots and Shoes,	103,	51 50
	W. H. Sampson, for relief of app. No. 173,	104,	10 00
	Richards & Gooch, Mdse., Groceries,	105,	52 50
28—	Wm. Peters, for relief of app. No. 414,	106,	10 00
	Norton & Co., Mdse., Flour,	107,	65 00
29—	R. H. Mason, Mdse., Stoves,	108,	212 60
	J. W. Stearns & Sons, Mdse., Groceries,	109,	82 56
	A Brother, app. No. 428,	110,	15 00
	Hartwell Bros., Mdse., Fuel,	111,	245 00
	Wm. Peters, Labor acct., Services	112,	60 00
	J. Morison, " " "	113,	100 00
	W. H. Davenport " " "	114,	78 00
	Jno. P. Ferns, " " "	115,	52 00
	H. Duvall, " " "	116,	100 00
Dec. 1—	J. Barry, for relief of app. No. 75,	117,	12 00

MASONIC BOARD OF RELIEF.

Date.	To whom paid, and on what account.	No. Voucher.	Amt.
Dec. 1	A Brother, app. No. 451,	118,	$150 00
2	Field, Leiter & Co., Mdse., Dry Goods,	119,	554 50
	W. W. Strong, Mdse., Furniture,	120,	118 95
4	G. S. Richardson & Co., Mdse., Boots and Shoes,	121,	48 90
	A. V. Morton, Mdse., Dry Goods,	122,	10 30
6	Colby & Wirts, Mdse., Furniture,	123,	73 64
7	C. G. Udell, Mdse., Ladders,	124,	14 67
	J. V. Farwell & Co., Mdse., Dry Goods,	125,	45 50
9	W. W. Strong, Mdse., Furniture,	126,	105 60
11	G. S. Richardson & Co., Mdse., Boots and Shoes,	127,	34 50
13	K. M. Kossar, for relief of app. No. 304,	128,	30 00
	Reno & Little, Mdse., Fuel,	129,	70 50
	H. Phillips, Mdse., Groceries,	130,	72 00
14	John L. Davies & Co., Mdse., Groceries,	131,	28 00
	Clement, Morton & Co., Mdse., Clothing,	132,	895 75
	J. Morison, Supt., Mdse., Cash expended for supplies,	133,	117 70
15	Field, Leiter & Co., Mdse., Dry Goods,	134,	134 92
	Norton & Co., Mdse., Flour,	135,	91 00
	John E. Pettibone, Mdse., Paper Bags,	136,	16 20
	W. W. Strong, Mdse., Furniture,	137,	105 60
19	J. Friedman, for relief of app. No. 474,	138,	25 00
	R. H. Mason, Mdse., Stoves,	139,	218 30
20	A. Woolner, Mdse., Crockery,	140,	50 25
	M. Bookbinder, Mdse., Crockery,	141,	19 00
21	Jos. Magee, for relief of app. No. 130,	142,	15 00
	Field, Leiter & Co., Mdse., Dry Goods	143,	74 78
	Mead & Higgins, Mdse., Groceries,	144,	86 85
	Rand, McNally & Co., Expense acct., Printing,	145,	69 25
	Hartwell Bros., Mdse., Fuel,	146,	340 25
22	Wm. Gough, for relief of app. No. 153,	147,	8 00
	A. L. Hale & Bro., Mdse., Furniture,	148,	513 10
23	W. W. Strong, Mdse., Furniture,	149,	63 85
	J. Morison, Supt., Mdse., Cash expended for supplies,	150.	102 90
27	W. H. Sampson, for relief of app. No. 173,	151,	10 00
28	John L. Davies & Co., Mdse., Groceries,	152,	28 00
	Pick & Chladec, Mdse., Crockery,	153,	14 00
29	W. H. Lamb, for relief of app. No. 160,	154,	10 00
	W. H. Davenport, Labor acct., Services,	155,	78 00
30	Wm. Peters, " " "	156,	78 00
	Jno. P. Ferns, " " "	157,	52 00
	J. Morison, " " "	158,	100 00
	H. Duvall, " " "	159,	100 00
	Richards & Gooch, Mdse., Groceries,	160,	53 59
	W. W. Strong, Mdse., Furniture,	161,	60 75

11

Date.	To whom paid, and on what account.	No. Voucher.	Amt.
1872.			
Jan. 1—	D. R. Dyche & Co., for relief of app. No. 456, ... 162,		5 00
	S. H. Lasher, for relief of app. No. 418, ... 163,		20 00
	Colby & Wirts, Mdse., Furniture, ... 164,		19 44
3—	G. S. Richardson & Co., Mdse., Boots and Shoes, ... 165,		46 50
	Norton & Co., Mdse., Flour, ... 166,		104 00
	Heath & Milligan, for relief of app. No. 163, ... 167,		10 50
4—	Tillotson Bros., Mdse., Stoves, ... 168,		23 00
	Wm. Peters, for relief of app. No. 355, ... 169,		5 00
6—	R. H. Mason, Mdse., Stoves, ... 170,		140 00
9—	E. J. Hill, for relief of app. No. 517, ... 171,		8 00
	John Lyons, for relief of app. No. 500, ... 172,		29 50
	H. Phillips, Mdse., Groceries, ... 173,		59 10
	Mead & Higgins, Mdse., Groceries, ... 174,		62 60
	Field, Leiter & Co., Mdse., Dry Goods, ... 175,		518 58
	Norton & Co., Mdse., Flour, ... 176,		13 00
	J. Morison, Supt., Mdse., Cash expended for supplies, 177,		36 23
10—	Soper, Brainard & Co., for relief of app. No. 500, ... 178,		30 00
	J. Giller, for relief of app. No. 1, ... 179,		13 00
	R. H. Mason, Mdse., Stoves,, ... 180,		38 60
11—	J. W. Ellis, Cash sent for I. O. of O. F., ... 181,		25 00
13—	Noble & Little, for relief of app. No. 202, ... 182,		25 00
	Norton, Cole & Co., Mdse., Flour, ... 183,		32 50
	W. W. Strong, Mdse., Furniture, ... 184,		96 85
15—	McLean & Collins, Mdse., Stoves, ... 185,		15 00
	J. Morison, Labor acct., Services, ... 186,		50 00
	H. Duvall, " " " ... 187,		50 00
	W. H. Davenport, " " " ... 188,		39 00
	Wm. Peters, " " " ... 189,		39 00
	John P. Ferns, " " " ... 190,		26 00
16—	H. C. Wentworth, for relief of app. No. 380, ... 191,		11 00
18—	E. B. Ives, for relief of app. No. 540, ... 192,		15 00
19—	Reno & Little, for relief of app. No. 335, ... 193,		25 00
20—	Hall's S. & L. Co., Mdse., Hardware, ... 194,		133 00
	W. W. Strong, Mdse., Furniture, ... 195,		58 65
22—	Geo. R. McClellan, for relief of app. No. 499, ... 196,		30 00
23—	Jos. Magee, for relief of app. No. 130, ... 197,		15 00
	Norton, Cole & Co., Mdse., Flour, ... 198,		26 00
	J. Morison, Supt., Mdse., Cash expended for supplies, 199,		118 36
24—	E. E. Law, for relief of app. No. 528, ... 200,		8 00
25—	Noble & Little, for relief of app. No. 113, ... 201,		43 50
	Richards & Gooch, Mdse., Groceries, ... 202,		61 08
26—	Jonathan Clark, Mdse., Shelving, ... 203,		48 32
	W. H. Sampson & Co., for relief of app. No. 173, .. 204,		10 00

MASONIC BOARD OF RELIEF.   99

Date.	To whom paid, and on what account.	No. Voucher.	Amt.
Jan. 30—	Thos. Gough, for relief of app. No. 153,	205,	$ 8 00
	J. Morison, Supt., Mdse., Cash expended for supplies,	206,	19 65
31—	T. M. Vancourt, for relief of app. No. 545,	207,	30 43
	H. Phillips, Mdse., Groceries,	208,	63 08
	Field, Leiter & Co., Mdse., Dry Goods,	209,	53 34
	John L. Davies & Co., Mdse., Groceries,	210,	56 00
	Mead & Higgins, Mdse., Groceries,	211,	259 34
Feb. 1—	W. W. Strong, Mdse., Furniture,	212,	20 00
	J. Morison, Labor acct., Services,	213,	50 00
	H. Duvall, " " "	214,	50 00
	W. H. Davenport, " " "	215,	39 00
	Wm. Peters, " " "	216,	39 00
	J. P. Ferns, " " "	217,	26 00
2—	J. W. Stearns & Sons, Mdse., Groceries,	218,	36 68
3—	Cleveland Lodge, No. 211, Expense acc't, Office rent,	219,	75 00
	Norton, Cole & Co., Mdse., Flour,	220,	97 50
	J. Morison, Supt., Mdse., Cash expended for supplies,	221,	78 60
	W. W. Strong, Mdse., Furniture,	222,	30 95
6—	G. S. Richardson & Co., Mdse., Boots and Shoes,	223,	41 75
	Ed. Cook, for relief of app. No. 557,	224,	32 00
	Snyder & Lee, Expense acc't, Office rent,	225,	83 33
7—	John Buckley, Mdse., Stove,	226,	18 00
	C. H. Harrison, for relief of app. No. 565,	227,	20 00
	Clement, Morton & Co., Mdse., Clothing,	228,	97 50
8—	T. M. Fox, for relief of app. No. 473,	229,	25 00
10—	Wm. Peters, for relief of app, No. 414,	230,	25 00
	Norton, Cole & Co., Mdse., Flour,	231,	26 00
	W. W. Strong, Mdse., Furniture,	232,	46 05
14—	John D. Davies & Co., Mdse., Groceries,	233,	56 00
15—	J. Morison, Labor acc't, Services,	234,	50 00
	H. Duvall, " " "	235,	50 00
	W. H. Davenport, " " "	236,	39 00
	Wm. Peters, " " "	237,	39 00
	John P. Ferns, " " "	238,	26 00
17—	W. W. Strong, Mdse., Furniture,	239,	40 55
20—	E. A. Walkup, for relief of app. No. 437,	240,	22 50
	Hartwell Bros., Mdse., Fuel,	241,	942 00
	A. L. Hale & Bro., Mdse., Furniture,	242,	162 20
	J. Morison, Supt., Mdse., Cash expended for supplies,	243,	96 50
	Field, Leiter & Co., Mdse., Dry Goods,	244,	396 64
21—	G. Krischton, for relief of app. No. 355,	245,	35 00
	Richards & Gooch, Mdse., Groceries,	246,	91 03
22—	Norton, Cole & Co., Mdse., Flour,	247,	32 50
23—	Jos. Magee, for relief of app. No. 130,	248,	15 00

FINAL REPORT OF THE

Date.	To whom paid, and on what account.	No. Voucher.	Amt.
Feb. 23—	H. Phillips, Mdse., Groceries.	249,	$151 13
	Mead & Higgins, Mdse., Groceries.	250,	140 45
	Clement, Morton & Co., Mdse., Clothing,	251,	69 00
24—	Wm. Gough, for relief of app. No. 153,	252,	8 00
	W. W. Strong, Mdse., Furniture,	253,	17 55
28—	Norton, Cole & Co., Mdse., Flour,	254,	33 00
	W. H. Sampson, for relief of app. No. 173,	255,	10 00
29—	D. P. Wilson, for relief of app. No. 578,	256,	9 00
Mar. 1—	J. Morison, Supt., Mdse., Cash expended for supplies,	257,	83 15
	J. Morison, Labor acc't, Services,	258,	50 00
	H. Duvall, " " "	259,	50 00
	W. H. Davenport, " " "	260,	39 00
	Wm. Peters, " " "	261,	18 00
	John P. Ferns, " " "	262,	26 00
	Jennings, Expense acc't, Gas bill,	263,	6 39
2—	W. W. Strong, Mdse., Furniture,	264,	18 60
4—	Dr. Powell, Medical Services, for app. No. 167,	265,	30 00
6—	J. Morison, for relief of app. No. 414,	266,	25 00
7—	Mary Kruse, for relief of app. No. 602,	267,	25 00
	Snyder & Lee, Expense acc't, Office rent,	268,	83 33
	Norton, Cole & Co., Mdse., Flour,	269,	74 25
9—	D. A. Cashman, Expense acc't, Printing,	270,	32 50
11—	T. M. Fox, for relief of app. No. 473,	271,	25 00
12—	John L. Davies & Co., Mdse., Groceries,	272,	56 00
	G. S. Richardson & Co., Mdse., Boots and Shoes,	273,	39 50
	W. W. Strong, Mdse., Furniture,	274,	17 00
13—	J. Morison, for relief of app. No. 585,	275,	50 00
14—	Ann Wilson, for relief of app. No. 572,	276,	20 00
	E. B. Ives, for relief of app. No. 540,	277,	15 00
15—	C. Toops, for relief of app. No. 525,	278,	16 50
16—	Norton, Cole & Co., Mdse., Flour,	279,	26 75
	Richards & Gooch, Mdse., Groceries,	280,	59 57
	J. Morison, Labor acc't, Services,	281,	50 00
	H. Duvall, " " "	282,	50 00
	W. H. Davenport, " " "	283,	39 00
	John P. Ferns, " " "	284,	26 00
	W. W. Strong, Mdse., Furniture,	285,	26 60
	E. A. Walkup, for relief of app. No. 437,	286,	22 50
	M. Bookbinder, Mdse., Crockery,	287,	29 50
18—	Dr. C. F. Hart, Medical Services, for app. No. 167,	288,	12 50
20—	M. Spaulding, for relief of app. No. 616,	289,	25 00
	S. H. Lasher, " " 418,	290,	20 00
	John P. Ferns, " " 418,	291,	12 50
21—	Collins & Burgie, Mdse., Stoves,	292,	197 85

MASONIC BOARD OF RELIEF.

Date.	To whom paid, and on what account.	No. Voucher.	Amt.
Mar. 22—	Wm. Gough, for relief of app. No. 153,	293,	8 00
23—	Hartwell Bros., Mdse., Fuel,	294,	461 00
	J. Morison, Supt., Mdse., Cash expended for supplies,	295,	77 91
	H. Phillips, Mdse., Groceries,	296,	104 52
	Mead & Higgins, Mdse., Groceries,	297,	240 44
	Field, Leiter & Co., Mdse., Dry Goods,	298,	139 42
	M. B. Stubs, for relief of app. No. 600,	299,	25 00
	W. H. Davenport, Labor acc't, Services,	300,	22 58
28—	K. Dalton, for relief of app. No. 508,	301,	30 00
29—	W. H. Sampson & Co., for relief of app. No. 173,	302,	10 00
	Dr. G. G. Goll, Medical services, for app. No. 437,	303,	42 65
30—	Jos. Magee, for relief of app. No. 130,	304,	15 00
	J. Morison, Labor acc't, Services,	305,	50 00
	H. Duvall, " " "	306,	50 00
	J. P. Ferns, " " "	307,	26 00
	J. J. French, " " "	308,	12 00
Apl. 1—	Jamieson & Morse, Expense acc't, Printing,	309,	26 50
2—	Norton, Cole & Co., Mdse., Flour,	310,	20 25
5—	Pick & Chaladec, Mdse., Crockery,	311,	9 00
	S. D. Childs, Jr., & Co., Expense acc't, Seal,	312,	15 00
	Snyder & Lee, Expense acc't, Office rent,	313,	83 33
	J. Morison, Supt., Mdse., Cash expended for supplies,	314,	78 30
7—	H. Horner, for relief of app. No. 77,	315,	4 10
9—	J. Morison, Supt., Mdse., Cash expended for supplies,	316,	93 90
10—	R. H. Mason, Mdse., Stoves,	317,	52 50
11—	Field, Leiter & Co., Mdse., Dry Goods,	318,	110 10
	Mead & Higgins, Mdse., Groceries,	319,	66 91
	H. Phillips, Mdse., Groceries,	320,	71 40
13—	W. W. Strong, Mdse., Furniture,	321,	18 95
15—	J. Morison, Labor acc't, Services,	322,	50 00
	H. Duvall, " " "	323,	50 00
	J. J. French, " " "	324,	39 00
	Jno. P. Ferns, " " "	325,	26 00
17—	Norton, Cole & Co., Mdse., Flour,	326,	33 75
	E. B. Ives, for relief of app. No. 540,	327,	15 00
	G. M. Holden, " " 540,	328,	4 80
19—	J. Morison, Supt., Mdse., Cash expended for supplies,	329,	176 00
22—	W. W. Strong, Mdse., Furniture,	330,	55 90
23—	C. J. Franks, for relief of app. No. 385,	331,	25 00
	F. H. Holcomb, Mdse., Stove,	332,	19 00
	J. J. French, for relief of app. No. 630,	333,	20 00
	Hartwell Bros., Mdse., Fuel,	334,	141 50
25—	Waubansia Lodge, No. 160, Chicago Lodge Charity Fund,	335,	100 00

FINAL REPORT OF THE

Date.	To whom paid, and on what account.	No. Voucher.	Amt.
Apl. 25	W. H. Sampson & Co., for relief of app. No. 173,	336,	$ 25 00
30	H. Dufour, " "	153, 337,	10 00
	J. Morison, Labor acc't, Services,	338,	50 00
	H. Duvall, " " "	339,	50 00
	J. J. French, " " "	340,	39 00
	Jno. P. Ferns, " " "	341,	26 00
May 2	John G. Hafner, for relief of app. No. 106,	342,	15 00
6	I. W. Congdon, " " 371,	343,	25 00
7	G. W. Gillett, Expense acc't, Hauling,	344,	20 00
8	W. M. Egan, Treas., Mdse., Dry Goods, purchased by J. H. Anthon, G. M., N. Y.,	345,	1000 00
	J. E. Otis, for relief of app. No. 440,	346,	30 00
	Cobb, Andrews & Co., for relief of app. No. 31,	347,	27 20
9	Collins & Burgie, Mdse., Stoves,	348,	93 80
11	Norton, Cole & Co., Mdse., Flour,	349,	36 50
13	J. Wright, for relief of Charity acc't,	350,	22 50
14	J. E. Cleveland, for relief of app. No. 506,	351,	19 50
15	J. Morison, Labor acc't, Services,	352,	50 00
	H. Duvall, " " "	353,	50 00
	Jno. P. Ferns," " "	354,	26 00
16	Dr. G. G. Goll, Medical Services, sundry app.,	355,	119 58
18	Stanton & Co., Mdse., Groceries,	356,	46 87
	J. Morison, Supt., Mdse., Cash expended for supplies,	357,	80 26
	J. C. D. Whitney, for relief of app. No. 636,	358,	50 00
	G. S. Richardson & Co., Mdse., Boots and Shoes,	359,	37 25
21	W. W. Strong, Mdse., Furniture,	360,	72 45
	Norton, Cole & Co., Mdse, Flour,	361,	15 00
	A. H. Powers, for attendance on app. No. 630,	362,	15 00
	James Wright, for funeral expense app. No. 153,	363,	58 70
22	J. Morison, Supt., Mdse., Cash expended for supplies,	364,	38 35
23	B. G. Hopkins & Co., Mdse., Clothing,	365,	35 00
	Pick & Chaladec, Mdse., Crockery,	366,	10 00
	Hartwell Bros., Mdse., Fuel,	367,	72 50
	I. W. Babcock, attendance on app. No. 634,	368,	6 00
24	M. Bookbinder, Mdse., Crockery,	369,	15 00
25	W. M. Egan, Treas., for relief of app. No. 637,	370,	114 75
	W. M. Egan, J. H. Miles and R. H. Foss, app. No. 638, Relief Com., R. A. Masons,	371,	948 50
28	H. Dufour, for relief of app. No. 153,	372,	10 00
	Snyder & Lee, Expense acc't, Office rent,	373,	166 66
29	Geo. Merrill, for relief of app. No. 173,	374,	30 00
30	J. Morison, Labor acc't, Services,	375,	50 00
	H. Duvall, " " "	376,	50 00
	Jno. P. Ferns, " " "	377,	28 00

MASONIC BOARD OF RELIEF. 103

Date.	To whom paid, and on what account.	No.	Voucher.	Amt.
May 31	M. A. Thayer, for relief of app. No. 639,	378,	$	50 00
	Hartwell Bros., Mdse., Fuel,	379,		5 50
	Norton, Cole & Co., Mdse., Flour,	380,		8 50
	Jno. P. Ferns, for relief of Charity acc't,	381,		35 00
	Watson Bros., for relief of app. No. 77,	382,		3 75
	J. Morison, Supt., Mdse., Cash expended for supplies,	383,		13 80
	Dr. G. G. Goll, Medical attendance, app. No. 77,	384,		26 25
	J. A. Cleveland, for relief of app. No. 506,	385,		9 75
	J. E. Church, " " 420,	386,		35 00
	Hartwell Bros., Mdse., Fuel,	387,		9 00
	E. Gutzch, for relief of app. No. 551,	388,		18 00
	H. P. Stanwood, for relief of app. No. 506,	389,		3 00
	Dallas City Lodge, No. 235, part of Surplus ret'd,	390,		25 00
	H. Duvall, for relief of app. No. 631,	391,		146 30
June 20	M. M.'s Daughter, app. No. 640,	392,		25 00
	A. H. Powers, attendance on app. No. 631,	393,		2 75
24	J. Morison, Labor acc't, Services,	394,		80 00
	H. Duvall, " " "	395,		80 00
	E. N. Tucker, for relief of app. No. 631,	396,		39 00
	J. Morison, " " 641,	397,		6 55
25	Stanton & Co., Mdse., Groceries,	398,		12 03
	J. Morison, Labor acc't, Extra Services,	399,		100 00
	M. M.'s Widow, app. No. 642,	400,		50 00
	I. W. Congdon, for relief of app. No. 371,	401,		50 00
	S. Goldston, " " 643,	402,		28 00
27	E. St. John, " " 644,	403,		29 75
28	Collins & Burgie, Mdse., Stoves,	404,		24 20
	Jno. P. Ferns, Labor acc't, Extra Services,	405,		100 00
29	M. M.'s Widow, app. No. 312,	406,		25 00
July 2	P. Gas L. and C. Co., Expense acc't, Gas bill,	407,		4 08
24	D. A. Cashman, Expense acc't, Printing,	408,		10 00
	H. Duvall, Expense acc't, Cash p'd for sundry items.	409,		22 61
	H. Duvall, Labor acc't, Services,	410,		100 00
	H. Duvall, " " Extra Services,	411,		200 00
	Jos. Warren Lodge, Mass., prop'n of surplus, ret'd,	412,		124 93
	United Brethren " " " " "	413,		57 50
	Plymouth " " " " "	414,		109 14
	Holland Lodge, No. 8, N.Y., prop'n surplus ret'd.	415,		267 44
	Rising Star " No. 45, " " " "	416,		162 36
	Merchants " No. 709, " " " "	417,		301 27
	Solomon's " No. 196, " " " "	418,		70 00
	Greenwood " No. 569, " " " "	419,		53 00
	Gloversville " No. 429, " " " "	420,		226 50
	Madison " No. 93, N. J., " " "	421,		118 00

FINAL REPORT OF THE

Date.	To whom paid, and on what account.					No. Voucher.	Amt.
July 24—	Capital	"	No. 3, Neb.,prop'n surplus ret'd			-422,	$227 50
	LaFayette	"	No. 100, Conn.,	"	"	" -423,	181 00
	Hartford	"	No. 88,	"	"	" -424,	181 00
	St. John's	"	No. 4,	"	"	" -425,	181 00
	Friendship	"	No. 7, Ill.,	"	"	" -426,	64 00
	Stratton	"	No. 408,	"	"	" -427,	25 00
	Odell	"	No. 401,	"	"	" -428,	35 00
	Chesterfield	"	No. 445,	"	"	" -429,	30 00
	Chatsworth	"	No. 539,	"	"	" -430,	79 13
	Jerseyville	"	No. 394,	"	"	" -431,	35 25
	Doric	"	No. 319,	"	"	" -432,	89 50
	Virden	"	No. 161,	"	"	" -433,	60 00
	Old Time	"	No. 629,	"	"	" -434,	25 00
	Toulon	"	No. 93,	"	"	" -435,	15 00
	Trio	"	No. 57,	"	"	" -436,	75 00
	Perry	"	No. 95,	"	"	" -437,	35 00
	Tolono	"	No. 391,	"	"	" -438,	27 75
	Louisville	"	No. 196,	"	"	" -439,	38 87
	Bunker Hill	"	No. 151,	"	"	" -440,	37 50
	Dallas City	"	No. 235,	"	"	" -441,	25 00
	Kankakee	"	No. 389,	"	"	" -442,	79 25

Ashlar Lodge, No. 308, Ill., Chicago Lodge Charity Fund,--443,-- 972 00
Apollo Lodge, No. 642, Ill., Chicago Lodge Charity Fund,--444,-- 380 00
D. C. Cregier Lodge, No. 643, Ill., Chicago Lodge Charity Fund,------------------------------445,-- 379 50
Kilwinning Lodge, No. 311, Ill., Chicago Lodge Charity Fund,------------------------------446,--1540 00
Waubansia Lodge, No. 160, Ill., Chicago Lodge Charity Fund,------------------------------447,--1180 00
Landmark Lodge, No. 422, Ill., Chicago Lodge Charity Fund,------------------------------448,-- 276 00
Blair Lodge, No. 393, Ill., Chicago Lodge Charity Fund,--449,--1280 00
Cleveland Lodge, No. 211, Ill., Chicago Lodge Charity Fund,--------------------------------450,-- 954 00
Home Lodge, No. 508, Ill., Chicago Lodge Charity Fund,--451,-- 624 00
Chicago Lodge, No. 437, Ill., Chicago Lodge Charity Fund,--------------------------------452,--1116 00
Dearborn Lodge, No. 310, Ill., Chicago Lodge Charity Fund,------------------------------453,--1288 00

MASONIC BOARD OF RELIEF. 105

| Date. | To whom paid, and on what account. | No. Voucher. | Amt. |

July 24—Union Park Lodge, No. 610, Ill., Chicago Lodge
    Charity Fund,------------------------------------454,---8450 00
  Hesperia Lodge, No. 411, Ill., Chicago Lodge Charity Fund,--------------------------------------455,-- 536 00
  Garden City Lodge, No. 141, Ill., Chicago Lodge
    Charity Fund,------------------------------------456,--1368 00
  Herder Lodge, No. 669, Ill., Chicago Lodge Charity
    Fund,---457,-- 133 00
  Blaney Lodge, No. 271, Ill., Chicago Lodge Charity
    Fund,---458,--1216 00
 27—Wm. B. Warren Lodge, No. 209, Ill., Chicago
    Lodge Charity Fund, --------------------------459,--1408 00
  Covenant Lodge, No. 526, Ill., Chicago Lodge Charity Fund, --------------------------------------460,--1168 00
  Keystone Lodge, No. 639, Ill., Chicago Lodge Charity Fund--461,-- 468 00
Aug. 2—Pleiades Lodge, No. 478, Ill., Chicago Lodge Charity Fund,------------------------------------462,-- 536 00
  W. A. Butters & Co., Expense acc't, Com. on sales,-463,-- 49 18
  8—Thos. J. Turner Lodge, No. 409, Ill., Chicago
    Lodge Charity Fund, -------------------------464,-- 880 00
  Lessing Lodge, No. 557, Ill., Chicago Lodge Charity
    Fund, --465,-- 335 50
 10—Norton, Cole & Co., Expense acc't,----------------466,-- 8 00
  Oriental Lodge, No. 33, Ill., Chicago Lodge Charity
    Fund,---467,--1758 00
 13—Wyoming Chapter, O. E. S., No. 52, Ill., prop'n surplus ret'd, ----------------------------------468,-- 30 00
  Masters Lodge, No. 5, N. Y., prop'n surplus ret'd--469,-- 124 92
  Ind. Royal Arch Lodge, No. 2, N. Y., prop'n surplus
    ret'd,---470,-- 124 92
  Montauk Lodge, No. 286, N.Y., prop'n surplus ret'd-471,-- 124 92
  St. John's " No. 219, Pa., "   "   " -472,-- 124 80
  Shekinah " No. 246, Pa., "   "   " -473,-- 124 80
 14—Lincoln Park Lodge, No. 611, Ill., Chicago Lodge
    Charity Fund,------------------------------------474,-- 693 00
  Waldeck Lodge, No. 674, Ill., Chicago Lodge Charity Fund,---475,-- 126 00
  J. J. French, Labor acc't, Services,------------------476,-- 24 00
 15—Grand Lodge of New York, proportion of surplus returned to Jurisdictions,--------------------477,--3404 17
  Grand Lodge of Pennsylvania, proportion of surplus
    returned to Jurisdictions, ----------------------478,--2150 40

12

FINAL REPORT OF THE

Date.	To whom paid, and on what account.	No. Voucher.	Amt.
Aug. 14	Grand Lodge of Massachusetts, proportion of surplus returned to Jurisdictions,	479,	$1683 07
	Grand Lodge of Indiana, proportion of surplus returned to Jurisdictions,	480,	266 00
	Grand Lodge of Maine, proportion of surplus returned to Jurisdictions,	481,	112 00
	Grand Lodge of New Jersey, proportion of surplus returned to Jurisdictions,	482	1080 00
	Grand Lodge of California, proportion of surplus returned to Jurisdictions,	483,	1874 00
	Grand Lodge of Ohio, proportion of surplus returned to Jurisdictions,	484,	174 00
	Grand Lodge of Connecticut, proportion of surplus returned to Jurisdictions,	485,	332 00
	Grand Lodge of Kentucky, proportion of surplus returned to Jurisdictions,	486,	496 00
	Grand Lodge of Nebraska, proportion of surplus returned to Jurisdictions,	487,	114 00
	Grand Lodge of Nevada, proportion of surplus returned to Jurisdictions,	488,	138 00
	Grand Lodge of District of Columbia, proportion of surplus returned to Jurisdictions,	489,	756 00
	Grand Lodge of Missouri, proportion of surplus returned to Jurisdictions,	490,	362 00
	Grand Lodge of Kansas, proportion of surplus returned to Jurisdictions,	491,	190 00
	Grand Lodge of Louisiana, proportion of surplus returned to Jurisdictions,	492,	100 00
	Grand Lodge of New Foundland, proportion of surplus returned to Jurisdictions,	493,	116 00
	Grand Lodge of Quebec, proportion of surplus returned to Jurisdictions,	494,	170 00
	Grand Lodge of Canada, proportion of surplus returned to Jurisdictions,	495,	994 00
	Grand Chapter of Iowa, proportion of surplus returned to Jurisdictions,	496,	220 00
	Grand Lodge of Iowa, proportion of surplus returned to Jurisdictions,	497,	204 00
	Grand Lodge of Illinois, proportion of surplus returned to Jurisdictions,	498,	3028 00
16	H. W. Bigelow Lodge. No. 483, Ill., Chicago Lodge Charity Fund,	499,	972 00
	D. A. Cashman, Expense acc't, Printing,	500,	5 00

| Date. | To whom paid, and on what account. | No. Voucher. | Amt. |

Aug. 19—Germania Lodge, No. 182, Ill., Chicago Lodge
    Charity Fund, ---------------------------------- 501,- $1320 00
21—Mithra Lodge, No. 410, Ill., Chicago Lodge Charity
    Fund, -- 502,-- 780 00
22—The Panama Lodges, proportion of surplus returned
    to Jurisdictions, ------------------------------ 503,-- 146 00
26—National Lodge, No. 596, Ill., Chicago Lodge Char-
    ity Fund, -------------------------------------- 504,-- 415 00
30—H. Duvall, Labor acc't, Services, --------------- 505,-- 120 00
    H. Duvall, Expense acc't, Cash p'd for sundry items, 506,--   4 90
31—Accordia Lodge, No. 277, Ill., Chicago Lodge Char-
    ity Fund, -------------------------------------- 507,-- 760 00
Sept. 2—W. M. Egan, Discount on Draft on N. Y., ---- 508,--   10 00
    D. C. Cregier, per instruction of the Officers of the
    Grand Lodge of Quebec, ------------------------- 509,--   56 96
    Masonic Board of Relief, Chicago, (Permanent
    Board,) -- 510,- 6500 00

    Total, -- $83,049 63

GENERAL CASH ACCOUNT

Total amount received by D. C. Cregier, Pres't, ... $83,089 06
Total amount deposited with W. M. Egan, Treas., ... $83,089 06

SECRETARY'S CASH ACCOUNT.

RECEIPTS.

Total amount Checks drawn on Treasurer, ... $83,089 06
" " returned by applicants, and for Goods sold, ... 1,355 14

$84,444 20

DISBURSEMENTS.

Sundries for applicants, (rent, doctor bills, etc.,) ..... $	5,748 39
Groceries, Wooden Ware, etc., ...	4,043 16
Dry Goods, Clothing, etc., ...	5,994 98
Stoves, Hardware, etc., ...	2,913 03
Boots and Shoes, ...	692 40
Fuel, ...	2,727 15
Furniture, Crockery, etc., ...	2,321 96
Labor, ...	3,517 78
Expense, (Incidental,)	286 59
Advertising, ...	133 14
Printing and Stationery, ...	238 80
Postage Stamps, ...	46 19

MASONIC BOARD OF RELIEF. 109

Rent,	514 65
Protested Draft,	51 56
J. Seymour, to I. O. O. F.,	25 00
D. C. Cregier,	56 96
Chicago Lodges. (Charity Fund,)	25,412 00
Surplus Returned to Jurisdictions,	21,825 89
Chicago Masonic Board of Relief,	6,500 00
Amount left with D. C. Cregier, to pay for printing this Report, sending it to the donors, and expenses of Grand Masters invited to audit these accounts. Any remainder, after paying the above, is to be turned over to the Board of Relief,	1,394 57—884,444 20

RECAPITULATION.

Total amount Cash received,	883,089 06
" " Goods donated,	7,545 44
Total amount issued to Applicants,	830,631 37
" " Allotted to Chicago Lodges,	25,412 00
" " Surplus returned,	21,825 89
" " given to Chicago Masonic Board of Relief,	6,500 00
" " Paid on Sundry Accounts, Rent, Advertising, Printing and Stationery, Postage Stamps, Labor, etc.,	4,870 67
Balance left with D. C. Cregier, to pay for Printing Report, and Expense of Committee,	1,394 57
	890,634 50 890,634 50

TREASURER'S REPORT.

Total amount received of D. C. Cregier, Pres't, in
                Cash and Drafts,----------------$81,662 62
  "   "   received as premium on gold drafts,.   582 30
  "   "   received as interest on deposits, ...   844 14—$83,089 06

Total amount of checks paid, drawn by the President, and
                attested by the Secretary,--------------------$83,089 06

To account for the item of Interest, I call attention to the letter from the Officers of the Metropolitan National Bank, of New York.

Treasurer.

CHICAGO, Sept. 19th, 1872.

NEW YORK, Dec. 12, 1871.

W. M. EGAN, Esq., Treasurer.

Sir:—Your favor of the 9th inst., is received. It is not our custom to allow interest on deposits, but in consideration of the circumstances connected with your fund, we will allow you three per cent. on your balance, interest to commence December 15.

                    Respectfully Yours,
                          For G. I. SENEY,
                Cashier Metropolitan National Bank.
(Signed,)   H. A. CHAPIN, Jr.

STATEMENT OF DISTRIBUTIONS.

The following Tabulated Statement will show, in detail, the distribution of Supplies, etc., and to whom; also, the particulars concerning same.

A KEY EXPLAINING THE USE OF THE LETTERS IN THE REMARK COLUMN.

A—Represents, the applicant received all the aid asked for.
B—The applicant declined to receive the aid offered.
C—Of the aid asked for, a part only was granted.
D—Received aid until it was no longer required.
E—Received aid from this Board ; also, from the General Relief Society.
F—Continuance of aid declined, as, by investigation, the applicant was found not in need.
G—The applicant also received aid from the I. O. O. F. Relief Committee.
H—The applicant also received aid from the Police Relief Committee.
I—The applicant also received aid from the Fireman's Relief Committee.
J—The applicant, or some member of the family, was sick.
K—Denotes death of applicant, subsequent to application.
L—The applicant was not burned out, but claimed to be an indirect sufferer by the Fire.
N—When able, the applicant returned all or part of the aid given, to be re-distributed to others more needy.
O—Further aid was refused, because investigation showed that the applicant was not a sufferer by the Fire.
P—The applicant also received aid from other Relief Societies or Committees than those named above.
R—The applicant was found to be unworthy of further aid.
S—The application was refused, by action of the Full Board.
T—The application was refused, by application of the Executive Committee.
U—The applicant was not considered in need of the aid asked for; or, the investigation was not satisfactory.
V—Investigation proved that the party had no claim upon the Fraternity.
W—The applicant was not vouched for; or, was unable to prove that he was a Mason.

FINAL REPORT OF THE

No. of Application	Lodge and No.	Location	No. in Family	Widows & Children	Provisions	Fuel	Clothing	H. Goods & Furniture	Stoves	Med. Att. & Medic.	Board	Rent	Tools	Cash	Transportation	Other Aid	Insured	Letters Written	Investigations	Tickets Issued	Refused	Remarks	Total Amount Given
1	Covenant	526 Chicago	9	1	1	1	1					2					1			2	16	A. J.	$192 79
2	Non-affiliated		1		1	1												1		1		A.	4 50
3	Valley	109 N. Y.	1																	3		A.	19 90
4	Mithra	410 Chicago	2		1	1								1						2		A.	5 31
5	Harlem	540 Ill.	1		1	1	1													2		A.	4 50
6	H. W. Bigelow	438 Chicago	2			1												2	3	5		A.	34 50
7	Dearborn	310 do.	1			1														1		A.	4 50
8	Mateland	112 Canada	1																	3		A.	6 00
9	Non-Affiliated		2	1																2		A. J.	10 00
10	Michigan	50 Mich.	1																		1	Unworthy,	2 25
11	Hardin	29 Iowa	1																	3		A.	6 00
12	Germania	182 N. Y.	1											1						2		A.	6 00
13	Bowen	486 Ill.	1																	3		A.	32 00
14	Royal Standard	Canada	1																	3		A.	25 00
15	Garden City	141 Chicago	2	1	1															2		A.	6 45
16	Blaney	271 do.	2																	2		A.	68 00
17	Williamsburg	E. D. N. Y.	1															1		2		A.	6 00
18	Neptune	317 do.	1																	3		Unworthy	22 00
19	Garden City	141 Chicago	1																	2		A.	16 50
20	Colchester	626 Ill.	1																	2		A.	8 00
21	Unity	48 do.	2	1																4		A.	143 00
22	High Falls	428 N. Y.	1																	1		A.	18 90
23	T. J. Turner	409 Chicago	1											1					3	2		A.	15 50
24	Frontier City	422 N. Y.	2																	1		A.	17 00
25	Cleveland	211 Chicago	2		1	1	1							1					1	3		A.	56 00
26	Euphrates	257 England	1		1		1							1						4		A.	28 10

MASONIC BOARD OF RELIEF.

27	Atlanta	59	Ga.								A.		35 60
28	Phoenix	262	N.Y.							2	A.	1-1	22 00
29	St. Johns	26	Kansas							5	A.	1-1	63 00
30	Columbian	7	Ga.	3	1					3	A.	1-1	
31	Supreme Council		France							1	IB.	1-1	27 20
32	St. Peters	419	England	1	1					1	E. P. C.	1-1	27 00
33	Wm. B. Warren	209	Chicago	3	1	1	1			3	Sojourner, A.	1-3	56 67
34	T. J. Turner	309	do.	3	1	1	1			2-5	C. E.		13 60
35	St. Johns	51	Me.	4	1					1	A.	1-1	68 75
36	Waubansia	160	Chicago	6	1		1			5	A.	1-1	37 56
37	Garden City	141	do.	4	1	1				1	A.	1-1	26 53
38	Kilwinning	311	do.	4	1						A.		$22 00
39	Hampton	347	N.Y.	1	1					2	A.	1-1	17 18
40	Richmond	196	Ind.	2	1	1	1			4	A.	1-1	19 38
41	Dearborn	310	Chicago	2	1	1				3	A.	1-1	40 00
42	Oriental	33	do.	4	1	1				3	A.		100 00
43	Illyna		Ohio	4	1	1				3	A.		60 00
44	Ionic	486	N.Y.	1							A.		27 00
45	Accordia	277	Chicago	1	1	1		1	1	2	A.	1-2	4 50
46	St. Johns	3	Canada	1	1	1		1	1	1	A.	1-1	3 50
47	Germania	182	Chicago	8	1	1		1		1	A.	1-1	4 00
48	Kilwinning	311	do.	3	1	1		1		2	A.	1-2	8 55
49	Mithra	410	do.	2	1	1		1		1	A.	1-1	4 50
50	do.	410	do.	2	1	1		1		1	A.	1-1	4 88
51	Germania	182	do.	2	1		1	1		10	E. C.	3-10	100 19
52	Kilwinning	311	do.	4	1		1	1	1	3	F.	1-3	7 27
53	Keystone	639	do.	6	1		1	1	1	4	E. A.	1-4	16 05
54	Non-affiliated							1		8	E. F.	3-8	76 28
55	Keystone	639	Chicago	5	1	1		1	1	12	C.	2-12	71 72
56	do.	639	do.	6	1	1		1	1	2	E. A.	3-2	50 30
57	Zerubbabile	329	N.Y.	7	1	1		1	1	1	G. F.	1-1	7 45
58	Mithra	410	Chicago	2	1	1		1	1	3	A.	1-3	10 25
59	Mattoon	260	Ill.	1									

FINAL REPORT OF THE

No. of Application.	Lodge and No.	Location	Widows & Children.	No. in Family.	Provisions.	Fuel.	Clothing.	H. Goods & Furnit'e.	Stores.	Med. Att. & Medic.	Board.	Rent.	Tools.	Cash.	Transportation.	Other Aid.	Insured.	Letters Written.	Investigations.	Tickets Issued.	Refused.	Remarks	Total Amount Given.
60	Mount Zion	311 N.Y.		2		1		1											1	2		A.	$22 10
61	Perfect Ashlar	604 N.Y.		2			1								1				1	1		A.	22 00
62	Germania	182 Chicago		2			1												1	1		A.	3 50
63	Covenant	526 do.		2		1	1	1											1	4		A.	11 55
64	Accordia	277 do.		2			1												1	1		A.	17 50
65	Manahattan	489 N.Y.		3		1	1											1	1	1		A.	5 25
66	Mithra	410 Chicago		4	1	1	1	1	1	1								1	2	10		F.	80 46
67	Covenant	526 do.		4	1	1	1												2	2		E. A. N.	70 00
68	Prairie	77 Ill.		7																	1	B.	
69	Claypool	13 Iowa		3		1	1	1											1	6		A.	20 28
70	II. W. Bigelow	438 Chicago		6	1	1	1	1											1	5		H.F.	41 45
71	do.	438 do.		3		1	1	1											1	1		H.F.	40 12
72	Garden City	141 do.		4		1	1	1											1	1		I.F.	7 10
73	Middlin Pillar	19 Sweden		10	1	1	1	1	1	1								1	2	14		F.	86 78
74	Brownsville	60 Penn.		1	1	1	1												1			A.	11 00
75	Non-affiliated	827 Ireland		5	1	1	1			1							1		8	6		F.	26 55
76	Covenant	526 Chicago		3		1	1	1											1	1		A.	18 00
77	Germania	182 do.		7	1	1	1	1	1	1					1		1	1	35	35		A. J. K	365 30
78	do.	182 do.		3	1	1	1												9	9		F.	79 26
79	Kilwinning	311 do.		3	1	1	1			1									1	7		A. E.	76 21
80	Not known	Ill.		1	1	1	1												1	1		A.	118 00
81	Porter	137 Ind.		1	1	1	1												1	1		A.	17 60
82	Blaney	271 Chicago		4	1	1	1												1	8		A.	62 88
83	Non-affiliated			1																		A.	5 00
84	Waubansia	160 Chicago		2	1	1	1												2	3		A.	29 86
85	Cleveland	211 do.		2	1	1	1												2	2		A.	42 60

MASONIC BOARD OF RELIEF.

No.	Lodge	No.	Location													Initials	Amount
86	Ashlar	308	do.		1								1	1		A.	11 00
87	Fraternal	27	Ala.	8		1	1	1	1	1	1		2	1		E. F.	26 70
88	Garden City	141	Chicago	1		1	1	1	1		1		2	1		A. E.	6 50
89	do.	141	do.	2		1	1	1	1	1	1		5	6		A.	34 12
90	do.	141	do.	10		1	1	1	1		1		3	12		A. J.	94 01
91	do.	141	do.	4		1	1	1	1		1		1	3		F.	53 88
92	St. Johns	40	Canada	5		1	1	1	1	1	1		5	6		E. D. L.	68 98
93	Not known		Penn.	1	1	1	1	1	1	1	1		1	5		A. P.	39 50
94	Clybourne	293	Tenn.	4		1	1	1	1		1		1	1		A.	45 00
95	Blair	393	Chicago	2		1	1	1	1		1		1	6		A. L.	19 78
96	Garden City	141	do.			1	1	1	1	1	1		1	7		E. A. J.	35 05
97	Pythagoras	137	Canada	5	1	1	1	1	1		1		2	21		E. J. F.	114 46
98	Oriental	33	Chicago	2		1	1	1	1	1	1		1	2		N. A.	15 88
99	Belvidere	60	Ill.	2	1	1	1	1	1	2	1		2	7 12		E. J. C.	146 45
100	Waubansia	160	Chicago	3		1	1	1	1		1		2	12		A. J.	109 10
101	Garden City	141	do.	3		1	1	1	1		1			2	1 T.	F.	3 50
102	W. B. Warren	209	do.	3		1	1	1	1	1	1		1	2		A.	19 35
103	Hesperia	411	do.	2		1	1	1	1		1		2	3		A.	26 70
104	W. B. Warren	209	do.	2		1	1	1	1	1	1		1	3		A.	50 47
105	H. W. Bigelow	438	do.	7		1	1	1	1		1		2	4		A.	126 72
106	Covenant	526	do.	5		1	1	1	1	1	1		1	4		A. J.	7 61
107	Keystone	639	do.	2		1	1	1	1		1		1	2		A.	32 52
108	Kilwinning	311	do.	3	1	1	1	1	1		1		1	5		A. J. O.	54 91
109	do.	311	do.	5		1	1	1	1		1		1	8		C. F.	22 00
110	Wm. B. Warren	209	do.	2	1	1	1	1	1	1	1		1	1		A.	39 41
111	Darcey	187	N. Y.	2		1	1	1	1		1		1	4		A. G.	59 50
112	Kilwinning	311	Chicago	10		1	1	1	1	1	1		1	7		A. J.	202 74
113	Covenant	526	do.	5		1	1	1	1		1		2	17		A. P.	69 77
114	Cleveland	211	do.	4		1	1	1	1	1	1		1	4		A.	1 35
115	Darcey	187	N. Y.	1		1	1	1	1		1		1	1		C. D. E. J.	106 47
116	A. W. Rawson	145	Ill.	7		1	1	1	1	1	1	1	2	16		A. J.	11 50
117	Garden City	141	Chicago	2		1	1	1	1		1		2	4		A.	20 00
118	Sharon	116	Wis.	2		1	1	1	1		1		1	1			

No. of Application	Lodge and No.	Location	No. in Family	Widows & Children	Provisions	Fuel	Clothing	H. Goods & Furn'e.	Stoves	Med. Att. & Medic	Board	Rent	Tools	Cash	Transportation	Other Aid	Insured	Letters Written	Investigations	Tickets Issued	Refused	Remarks	Total Amount Given
119	Marion 35	Ind.	7				1	1								1			1	1		A. L.	$34 81
120	Accordia 277	Chicago	5				1	1											2	9		A.	96 57
121	Wheaton 269	Ill.	2				1												1	1		A.	16 00
122	Germania 182	Chicago	2		1	1	1	1											1	7		C. F.	45 78
123	do. 182	do.	2					1											1	4		A.	21 41
124	D. C. Cregier 643	do.	3					1							1	1		1		2		Unworthy	8 60
125	Chicago 437	do.	9		1	1	3	1								1	1		2	2		E. P. F.	34 17
126	River Falls 104	Wis.	1					1							1				2	4			7 60
127	Wm. B. Warren 209	Chicago	2			1	1	1								1			2	2		C. F.	28 30
128	Accordia 277	do.	6		1	1	1	1								1			2	3		A.	210 92
129	Mithra 410	do.	7			1	1	1								1		1	3	23		J. C. D.	54 28
130	Oriental 33	do.	3		1	1	3	1					4			1			2	6		A. P.	162 93
131	Mithra 410	do.	7		1	1	1	1								1			4	17		P. F. J.	127 72
132	Blair 393	do.	4					1								1			3	9		G. A.	11 05
133	Keystone 639	do.	4					1								1			5	3		F. E.	86 83
134	D. C. Cregier 643	do.	2		1	1		1								1			1	14		E. A.	44 50
135	Blair 393	do.	4					1							1	1		1				A.	52 54
136	Mithra 410	do.	5			1	1	1							1	1			6	6		A.	64 12
137	do. 410	do.	7		1		1	1								1			1	14		A. J.	111 48
138	Germania 182	do.	3			1	1	1							1	1			1	10		A.	52 42
139	do. 182	do.	3		1	1	1	1								1			1	9		C.	98 55
140	Keystone 639	do.	4					1								1			2	3		C.	20 50
141	do. 639	do.	2					1								1			2	3		A.	20 50
142	Mithra 410	do.	4			1	1	1								1			1	1			9 55
143	do. 410	do.	7				1	1								1			1	9		F.	64 77
144	Hesperia 411	do.	2		1	1	1	1								1		1	3	28		A. P.	231 84

MASONIC BOARD OF RELIEF.

No.	Lodge	No.	Location											Name	Amount
145	D. C. Cregier	643	Chicago	6		1	1					2	45	C. E. J.	205 78
146	Germania	182	do.	7		1	1					1	-7	Unworthy.	-59 15
147	Accordia	277	do.	8		1	1					2	-4	A.	-61 36
148	Mithra	410	do.	4		1	1					1	-7	E. A.	-29 73
149	do.	410	do.	5		1	1					1	.6	E. F.	-31 48
150	H. W. Bigelow	438	do.	3		1	1					2	-4		-39 23
151	Kilwinning	311	do.	2	1	1	1			1		1	-3	A. O.	-17 36
152	St. George	6	N. Y.	5		1	1					2	16	C. O.	-100 80
153	Old LaFayette	18	Chicago	3		1	1			1		1		D.	-278 29
154	Mithra	410	do.	2		1	1					3	43	A. J. K.	
155	Union	60	Md.	2		1	1	8				1		T.	-4 91
156	Covenant	526	Chicago	6	1	1	1					1	2	A. E. N.	-132 36
157	Germania	182	do.	6		1	1					3	15	F. E. J.	-38 79
158	Geneva	139	Ill.	2		1	1					2	.6	A.	-2 11
159	Cleveland	211	Chicago	4		1	1					2	.6	C.	-83 56
160	T. J. Turner	409	do.	3		1	1					2	12	F. G. E	-59 69
161	Kilwinning	311	do.	2		1	1					1	-4	A.	-24 61
162	Garden City	141	do.	6		1	1					1	-3	A.	-12 62
163	Lincoln Park	611	do.	4		1	1					2	-3	A. E.	-30 33
164	Orient Français	107	Mo.	1		1	1				7	3	12	E. F. C.	-88 41
165	St. Johns	19	Sweden	6		1	1					2	2	C. F.	-21 28
166	St. Andrews	62	Canada	2		1	1					1		A.	-66 00
167	T. J. Turner	409	Chicago	7		1	1					3	9	A. J.	-92 95
168	do.	409	do.	2		1	1					1	1	C. F.	-10 00
169	Blair	393	do.	2		1	1			1		1	1	A.	-8 65
170	H. W. Bigelow	438	do.	5		1	1					1	5	A.	-38 86
171	Kilwinning	311	do.	3		1	1					3	13	A.	-98 84
172	Unknown		Wis.	1	1	1	1					1	1	A.	-6 55
273	Wm. B. Warren	209	Chicago	2		1	1	1	1	2		4	32	C. E. J.	-256 68
174	Berlin	38	Wis.	6		1	1		1	1		2	2	C. F.	-23 00
175	Germania	182	Chicago	2		1	1					3	11	A. J.	-143 51
176	Wm. B. Warren	209	do.	4		1	1					2	-3	C. F.	-12 35
177	Garden City	141	do.	2		1	1					1	1	A.	-27 00

FINAL REPORT OF THE

No. of Application.	Lodge and No.		Location	No. in Family.	Provisions	Fuel	Clothing	H.Goods & Furniture	Stores	Med. Att. & Medic.	Board	Rent	Tools	Cash	Transportation	Other Aid	Insured	Letters Written	Investigations	Tickets Issued	Refused	Remarks	Total Amount Given
178	Lessing	557	Chicago	5	1		1	1									1	1	1	3		A.	$27 01
179	Winona	18	Minn.	2											1			1	2	4		A.	36 75
180	Golden Rule	159	Mich.	1	1		1	1							1				1	1		A.	11 00
181	Borough	637	England	1	1		1	1											1	1		C.	5 38
182	H. W. Bigelow	438	Chicago	8	1		1	1					1				1	1	3	5		A.	33 43
183	Accordia	277	do.	2					1								1		1	1		C.F.	28 81
184	California	1	Cal.	3	1		1	1											1	3		A.	9 56
185	Hesperia	411	Chicago	4	1		1	1							1				1	1		A.	16 00
186	Cleveland	211	do.	2			1										1		2	2		A.	48 00
187	Accordia	277	do.	1															1	1		A.	4 00
188	Garden City	141	do.	4	1		1	1									1		1	2		A.	22 03
189	Atlantic	178	N. Y.	4													1		1	2	1	Unworthy.	5 00
190	Adelphia	23	N. Y.	8	1		1	1							1	1	1	1	2	6		A.	35 07
191	Germania	182	Chicago	6	1		1	1									1		1	3		A.	13 26
192	do.	182	do.	3	1		1	1									1		2	4		A.	48 43
193	Waubansia	160	do.	3	1		1	1							1		1		2	7		F.	39 24
194	Germania	182	do.	2	1		1	1									1	1	2	6		A.	50 32
195	Athols	384	Scotland	5	1		1	1		1							1	1	1	14		F.	105 64
196	Kilwinning	311	Chicago	3			1										1		2	3		F.S.	6 67
197	do.	311	do.	10	1		1	1									1		2	4		A.	30 00
198	Dearborn	310	do.	4	1		1	1									1		2	5		A.	28 26
199	Waubansia	160	do.	3	1		1	1											3	13		F.G.	94 00
200	Tarbolton	351	Ill.	8	1		1	1							1		1		1	2		A.	109 75
201	Dublin		Ireland	4	1		1	1									1		1	1		A.	83 67
202	Unknown		do.	3													1	1	1	9		A.	143 10
203	Kilwinning	311	Chicago																				

MASONIC BOARD OF RELIEF.

#	Lodge	No.	Location									Code	Amount
204	Republican	325	N.Y.						3		1-3	A.	17 01
205	Ill. W. Bigelow	438	Chicago						2	1	1-17	A.	173 48
206	Germania	182	do.					1	1	1	1-1	A.	22 00
207	do.	182	do.					1	5	1	-4	Unworthy	36 80
208	Kilwinning	311	do.					1	5	1	3-7	A.	67 97
209	Horricon	244	Ill.					1	6	1	2 2	A.	28 05
210	Cleveland	211	Chicago					1	3	1	1-3	F. T.	18 30
211	Germania	182	do.				1	1	6	1	2-9	A. E. J.	30 17
212	Chicago	437	do.					1	4	1	3-7	D. G.	31 08
213	Germania	182	do.					1	3	1	1-8	A. J.	23 25
214	St. Johns	1	S.C.			1		1	2	1	3 13	A. E.	118 05
215	Accordia	277	Chicago					1	5	1	1-7	A.	51 15
216	Mithra	410	do.					1	7	1	1-1	A.	46 25
217	Germania	182	do.					1	8	1	2 30	A. J.	34 95
218	do.	182	do.			1		1	4	1	2 13	C. D.	250 30
219	Mountain	281	Penn.					1	4	1	1-2	A.	115 15
220	Victoria	11	Canada					1	1	1	3 21	D. C.	9 75
221	Chemung	258	Ill.					1	4	1	4 13	Impostor	169 09
222	Meridian	3	Iowa					1	2	1	1-1	S.	117 12
223	Not known								3		1-5	A.	24 05
224	Keystone	639	Chicago		1			1	6	1	2 20	A. J.	203 25
225	Cleveland	211	Chicago					1	0	1	1-9	F. H.	92 58
226	Covenant	526	do.					1	6	1	-4	A.	32 37
227	Germania	182	do.					1	3	1	3-4	C.	14 73
228	Accordia	277	do.					1	1	1	1-1	A.	16 90
229	Dearborn	310	do.				1	1	1	1	1-1	A.	24 00
230	Howard	69	Maine					1	2	1	-4	A.	18 08
231	Germania	182	Chicago					1	4	1	1-1	A.	11 00
232	Garden City	141	do.		1			1	1	1	1-5	A.	35 69
233	Germania	182	do.					1	5	1	3 20	D.	108 45
234	Mithra	410	do.					1	6	1	-4	D. J.	13 15
235	Union Park	610	do.					1	5	1	1-1	A.	14 2
236	Blair	393	do.					1		1	1-1	C.	

FINAL REPORT OF THE

No. of Application	Lodge and No.	Location	No. in Family	Widows & Children	Provisions	Fuel	Clothing	H. Goods & Furn't'e	Stoves	Med., Att., & Medic.	Board	Rent	Tools	Cash	Transportation	Other Aid	Insured	Letters Written	Investigations	Tickets Issued	Refused	Remarks	Total Amount Given
237	Alma	931 Canada	6					1			1		1						1	4		A.	$44 00
238	Germania	182 Chicago	7		1	1	1				1					1	1		2	7		D.	37 10
239	do	182 do	5		1	1	1						1						2	7		C.	49 33
240	Pequossette	Mass	4			1	1	1		2							1			6		A.	21 00
241	Lessing	557 Chicago			1	1	1	1										1	1	2	4		C.	24 25
242	Dearborn	310 do	2		1	1	1										1		2	7		A.	61 69
243	Eastern Star	227 N.Y.	2		1												1			4		A.	2 25
244	Wm. B. Warren	209 Chicago	5		1	1	1	1							1		1		1	13		A.	52 90
245	National	596 do	6		1	1	1	1								1	1		1	4		F. Unworthy	99 92
246	Wm. B. Warren	209 do	2			1	1										1		1	8		C. I.	40 36
247	do	209 do	2		1	1	1	1									1		1			A. J. P.	61 77
248	Covenant	526 do	4		1	1	1										1		1	6		S. Unworthy	54 76
249	Germania	182 do	7		1	1	1			1							1		1	5		A.	49 43
250	Hiram	50 Wis	2		1	1	1										1		1	5		D.	42 63
251	Germania	182 Chicago	5		1	1	1										1			10		C.	87 65
252	do	182 do	4		1	1	1										1			6		A.	53 59
253	Covenant	526 do	7		1	1	1										1			7		F.	49 63
254	Waubansia	160 do	2		1	1	1										1			5		A.	35 70
255	Germania	182 do	5		1	1	1						1				1			11		A.	50 00
256	do	182 do	5		1	1	1										1			9		F. Unworthy	57 83
257	Keystone	639 do	7		1	1	1										1			6		A.	66 81
258	Germania	182 do	5		1	1	1										1		1	11		T.	41 21
259	do	182 do																		2			A.	29 71
260	Geneva	139 Ill.	4		1	1	1										1		1	4		A.	57 94
261	Mithra	410 Chicago			1	1	1										1		1	7		C. D.	20 68
262	Covenant	526 do	3																				

MASONIC BOARD OF RELIEF.

No.	Lodge	No.	Location									Amount
263	Cleveland	211	do	-4	1	1	1	1	1	2	24	A. J.	134 53
264	do	211	do	-5	1	1	1	1	1	2	6	I. S.	
265	Germania	182	do	-3	1	1	1	1	1	1	1	C.	41 26
266	Lessing	557	do	-2	1	1	1	1	1	1	4	A.	-1 25
267	Germania	182	do	-2	1	1	1	1	1	1	1	A.	-37 15
268	D. C. Cregier	643	do	-5	1	1	1	1	1	-1	1	E. G. S.	
269	Germania	182	do	-3	1	1	1	1	1	2	17	D.	120 11
270	do	182	do	-6	1	1	1	1	1	3	25	D.	163 97
271	do	182	do	-1	1	1	1	1	1	3	8	D. E.	59 02
272	Accordia	277	do	-2	1	1	1	1	1	2	5	D.	-38 90
273	do	277	do	-4	1	1	1	1	1	1	1	A.	-5 50
274	Germania	182	do	-5	1	1	1	1	1	2	3	C. D.	-17 45
275	do	182	do	-4	1	1	1	1	1	2	5	A.	-53 57
276	Cleveland	211	do	-2	1	1	1	1	1	2	8	D.	-72 39
277	Germania	182	do	-6	1	1	1	1	1	1	4	C.	-38 12
278	Garden City	141	do	-7	1	1	1	1	1	1	1	A.	-43 00
279	Mithra	410	do	-3	1	1	1	1	1	5	4	A. E.	-25 78
280	Blair	393	do	-8	1	1	1	1	1	4	4	A. E.	-52 30
281	Franklin		Mass.	-2	1	1	1	1	1	1	1	A.	-4 60
282	Mithra	410	Chicago	-3	1	1	1	1	1	1	1	Unworthy. T. R.	-5 00
283	Garden City	141	do	-3	1	1	1	1	1	2	2	C.	20 00
284	Kilwinning	311	do	-1	1	1	1	1	1	1	6	A.	34 51
285	Blaney	271	do	-4	1	1	1	1	1	1	4	A.	43 81
286	do	271	do	-8	1	1	1	1	1	1	7	C. L. P.	69 00
287	do	271	do	-5	1	1	1	1	1	1	3	A.	27 50
288	Germania	182	do	-6	1	1	1	1	1	1	1	A.	23 52
289	do	182	do	-4	1	1	1	1	1	2	2	C.	20 75
290	Dunlop	321	Ill.	-2	1	1	1	1	1	1	3	P. A.	30 65
291	Dearborn	310	Chicago	-8	1	1	1	1	1	2	13	D.	90 62
292	Mithra	410	do	-3	1	1	1	1	1	1	6	A. E.	35 76
293	Waubansia	160	do	-4	1	1	1	1	1	1	5	A.	60 02
294	Germania	182	do	-3	1	1	1	1	1	2	6	C.	-35 33
295	Washington Centennial	14	D. C.	-6	1	1	1	1	1	1	3	A.	-20 87

122 FINAL REPORT OF THE

No. of Application	Lodge and No.		Location	No. in Family	Widows & Children	Provisions	Fuel	Clothing	H. Goods & Furn'e.	Stoves	Med. Att. & Medic.	Board	Rent	Tools	Cash	Transportation	Other Aid	Insured	Letters Written	Investigations	Tickets Issued	Refused	Remarks	Total Amount Given
296	Germania	182	Chicago	3														1		1		1	T. U.	$
297	Amwell	14	N. J.	4																2		1	S. U.	
298	Cleveland	211	Chicago	5																2		1	S. U.	
299	Napanee	9	Canada	4			1	1	1									1		1	6		D.	107 31
300	Advtum	640	N. Y.	5				1												1	2		A.	9 00
301	Germania	182	Chicago	7				1	1	1										1	4		F. P.	56 71
302	do	182	do	1																	1	1	S. Unworthy.	
303	Blair	393	Ind.	7					1										1	3	1		A. E.	11 18
304	M. L. McClelland	357	do	4				1	1				1						1	3	1		A.	30 00
305	H. W. Bigelow	438	Chicago	5				1	1				1			1		1	1	5		A.	61 80
306	T. J. Turner	409	do	5												1			1	1	1		A.	4 75
307	Kihwinning	311	do	7				1	1									1	1	3		D. O. P.	25 68
308	do	311	do	3				1											2	4	1		A.	43 50
309	Mithra	410	do	8			1	1	1	1								1	1	4		A.	68 53
310	Corinthian	488	N. Y.	6															1		1	1	C.	33 00
311	Rockford	102	Ill.	1															1			1	C.	25 60
312	Mithra	410	Chicago	1			1	1	1	1								1	1	3		C.	104 29
313	Herman	127	Cal.	5				1	1										1	8		A.	14 72
314	Waldeck	674	Chicago	4				1	1									1	2	3		C. E.	71 20
315	Germania	182	do	5				1	1	1						1		1	4	15		D. E.	120 22
316	Greenwich	467	N. Y.	5				1	1										2	3	1		A.	25 52
317	Garden City	141	Chicago	4				1	1										1	1		A.	19 63
318	Germania	182	do	5																2		1	R.	4 60
319	Covenant	526	do	4					1										1	1	3		A.	13 88
320	Germania	182	do	3				1	1										1	1	5		C.	44 88
321	Accordia	277	do	3																1	1	1	F. S.	4 50

MASONIC BOARD OF RELIEF.

No.	Lodge	No.	Location										Init.	Amount
322	Kankakee	389	Ill.							2	4	1	A. P.	53 59
323	Accordia	277	Chicago							5	1		A.	14 71
324	King Solomon	22	Canada							3	13		A. J.	129 68
325	Kilwinning	311	Chicago							3	1		B.	
326	Cleveland City	15	Ohio							2	1		T. O.	
327	Mithra	410	Chicago							4	6	1	A.	38 17
328	Kilwinning	311	do							9	10	1	A.	106 84
329	Atlas	360	N. Y.							2	1		S.	
330	Apollo	642	Chicago							9	3	1	A. G.	10 95
331	Keystone	639	do							4	2	1	E. R. Unworthy	7 75
332	Kilwinning	311	do							5	13	1	D. E.	115 24
333	Hohenlinden	56	N. Y.							6	2		I. U. T.	
334	Milwaukee		Wis.							4	1		T. U. R.	
335	Keystone	639	Chicago							5	15	2	D. J.	145 93
336	Oriental	33	do							4	1		R. T. G.	
337	Garden City	141	do							1	2	1	A.	6 75
338	Lessing	557	do							5	4	1	A.	42 15
339	Chicago	437	do							11	5	2	D. G.	68 64
340	Garden City	141	do							1	2	1	C. R.	5 25
341	Yokohama	1092	Japan							1	1	1	C.	11 85
342	Chemung	258	Ill.							4	5	1	D.	110 55
343	Covert	11	Neb.							1	15	1	A.	48 33
344	Germania	182	Chicago							9	5	1	A.	18 00
345	H. W. Bigelow	438	do							1	5	1	A.	65 08
346	Blair	393	do							3	8	1	A. E.	64 46
347	Covenant	526	Ill.							4	2	1	D.	33 03
348	Lockport	73	N. Y.							1	2		S. V.	
349	Kilwinning	311	Chicago							5	7	3	C.	82 73
350	Accordia	277	do							7	8	2	A.	99 42
351	Dutcher	193	Mich.							2	1	1	S. U.	11 00
352	Neptune	419	Scotland							1	2	1	A.	37 50
353	Schoolcraft	118	Mich.							2	6	2	A. E.	102 41
354	Kilwinning	311	Chicago							7	10	1	D. E.	

FINAL REPORT OF THE

No. of Application	Lodge and No.		Location	No. in Family	Widows & Children	Provisions	Fuel	Clothing	H.Goods & Furn're	Stores	Med, Att. & Medic.	Board	Rent	Tools	Cash	Transportation	Other Aid	Insured	Letters Written	Investigations	Tickets Issued	Refused	Remarks	Total Amount Given
355	Blair	393	Chicago	4		1	1	1	1	1	1			1	1			1		-5	20		D. J.	$193 28
356	Germania	182	do	4		1	1	1	1									1	1	1	4	1	A.	48 75
357	do	182	do	6		1	1	1	1									1		1	3			33 85
358	Keystone	639	do	9		1	1	1	1	1	1							1		5	3		C.	15 10
359	Kilwinning	311	do	7		1	1	1	1									1	1	1	6		G. R. T.	56 35
360	Germania	182	do	7		1	1	1	1									1		2				15 73
361	Chicago	437	do	1		1	1	1	1	1						1		1	1	3	6		C. D.	66 78
662	Toronto		Canada	3		1			1									1		1			A.	16 50
363	Mithra	410	Chicago	7		1	1	1	1		1						1	1		1	2		A.	22 80
364	Mt. Moriah	155	Penn.	5		1	1	1	1									1		1	3		E. R.	24 27
365	Keystone	639	Chicago	5		1	1	1	1									1		1	4		A.	39 73
366	Worth	210	N. Y.	2		1	1	1	1									1		2	5		A.	46 22
367	Blair	393	Chicago	2		1		1	1		1							1		1	1		A.	30 56
368	do	393	do	4																			I.S.U.	18 00
369	Kokomo		Ind.	4		1	1	1	1	1					1			1		2	2		C.	10 28
370	Union	9	Canada	1		1	1	1										1		2	14		A.	184 50
371	Covenant	526	Chicago	6		1	1	1	1	1								1		2	4		A. J.	12 60
372	Kilbourne	399	Scotland	1		1												1		4	8		A.	61 94
373	Germania	182	Chicago	4		1	1	1	1	1	1							1		1	5		A. E.	56 55
374	do	182	do	7		1	1	1	1									1		2	8		A.	94 64
375	do	182	do	3		1	1	1	1								1	1		2	3		A.	18 93
376	Not Known		N. Y.	4		1	1	1	1	1								1		2	5		C.	52 50
377	Germania	182	Chicago	3		1	1	1	1									1		1	4		A.	40 52
378	Lessing	557	do	3		1	1	1	1								1	1		1	1		L. R.	8 00
379	W. R. Warren	209	do	2		1	1	1	1									1		1	4		A.	39 03
380	H. W. Bigelow	438	do	1		1	1	1	1									1		1	4		A.	

MASONIC BOARD OF RELIEF.   125

No.	Name	Lodge No.	Location								Code	Amount
381	Lessing	608	N. Y.	2		1			3	4	C.	22 14
382	Garden City	141	Chicago	2		1	1		1	3	C.	22 10
383	South Park	662	do	1				1	1	10	O. T.	
384	Independent Royal Arch	2	N. Y.	1			1	1	1	1	C.	9 93
385	Mithra	410	Chicago	4		1	1	1	11	2 6	A. J.	164 31
386	Drei Hammern Halbertstadt		Germany	1		1	1		1		A.	46 21
387	Accordia	277	Chicago	2		1	1	1		5	A.	59 60
388	Mendota	176	Ill.	2	1	1	1	1	2	8	D. E.	55 79
389	Germania	182	Chicago	3		1	1	1	1		A.	35 42
390	Accordia	277	do	7		1	1	1	7	6	A.	83 96
391	Dearborn	310	do	1		1	1	1	1		T. U.	
392	Germania	182	do	2		1	1	1	9		A.	95 35
393	Union	78	Wis.	4		1	1	1	7		A.	96 01
394	Mithra	410	Chicago	4		1	1	1	4		A.	37 00
395	Germania	182	do	8		1	1	1	5		A.	41 02
396	Keystone	639	do	5		1	1	1	3		A.	30 75
397	Germania	182	do	4		1	1	1	2	2	A.	42 30
398	Kilwinning	311	do	4		1	1	1	2	3	A.	28 74
399	Covenant	526	do	7		1	1	1	2	3	C. D.	27 38
400	Kilwinning	311	do	7		1	1	1	1	11	B. J.	
401	Germania	182	do	4	1	1	1	1	2	2	A.	92 87
402	Not Known		Mich.	3 1	1		1	2	1		Unworthy. P.	66 00
403	Garden City	141	Chicago	7		1	1	1		1	A.	
404	Kilwinning	311	do	7		1	1	1	2		A.	41 05
405	D. C. Cregier	643	do	9		1	1	1	2	8	A.	14 88
406	Germania	182	do	4		1	1	1	1	5	A. J.	130 80
407	Lincoln Park	611	do	4		1	1	1		5	A.	46 02
408	Mithra	410	do	1		1	1	1	1		T. U.	50 85
409	National	596	do	6		1	1	1	1		A.	
410	Covenant	526	do	6		1	1	1	1	4	A.	14 58
411	Kilwinning	311	do	6		1	1	1		6	A. E. J	29 93
412	Covenant	526	do	2		1	1	1	2	6	A. E. J	44 98
413	Keystone	639	do	7		1	1	1	2	3	C.	31 40

FINAL REPORT OF THE

No. of Application	Lodge and No.		Location	No. in Family	Widows & Children	Provisions	Fuel	Clothing	H. Goods & Furn'e	Stoves	Med. Att. & Medic.	Board	Rent	Tools	Cash	Transportation	Other Aid	Insured	Letters Written	Investigations	Tickets Issued	Refused	Remarks	Total Amount Given
414	Oriental	33	Chicago	2	1	1	1	1	1		1										5		D. J.	$210 61
415	Hesperia	411	do	5										1						2	23		E. S.	
416	Lincoln Park	611	do	2															1	1	2		A.	18 18
417	Germania	182	do	4																1	2		A.	36 45
418	Waubansia	160	do	2									2							2	2		A. J.	208 97
419	Wm. B. Warren	209	do	1					1		1								1	2	19		Unworthy	47 50
420	Armour	186	N. Y.	6												1				4	13		A. J.	146 03
421	Mithra	410	Chicago	7																2	1		E. R. S.	5 50
422	Vitruvious	81	Ill.	6															1	1	1		A.	11 35
423	Wiley M. Egan	593	Ill.	6													1						T. U.	
424	Blair	393	Chicago	7																3	6		C. E.	58 89
425	Cleveland	211	do	5					1											3		1	B.	
426	Accordia	277	do	2																3	3		A. E.	55 46
427	Eureka	243	N. Y.	5														1	1	2	11		A. P.	70 80
428	Cleveland	211	Chicago	5																2	6		A.	71 62
429	Frontier	45	Wis.	4																2	6		R. S.	32 19
430	Chicago	437	Chicago	8																1	2		A.	15 75
431	Germania	182	do	3											1	1				2	8		I B.	
432	Wm. B. Warren	209	do	7																1	4		A.	86 79
433	Chicago	437	do	1																1	2		A. P.	41 53
434	National	596	do	4																1	2		A.	48 00
435	Keystone	639	do	2									2							2	10		A. J. P. K.	98 41
436	Chicago	437	do	7																4	11		A. J. P. K.	160 83
437	Kilwinning	311	do	7																5	27		C. J. D.	289 62
438	Herder	669	do	2																1	1		A. G.	13 50
439	Amity	323	N. Y.	2																1	2		A. E.	14 48

MASONIC BOARD OF RELIEF. 127

440	Waubansia	160	Chicago	2	1				2	7	A. E.	82 78
441	Garden City	141	do	1	1				1	1	A. I.	4 60
442	Durand	302	do	3	1				2	2	C.	10 65
443	Fulton	216	Ga.	3	1			1	1	16	A. P.	133 03
444	Cleveland	211	Chicago	4	1				1	1	C.	9 00
445	Mithra (Orphans)	410	do	1	1				2	3	A.	65 74
446	LaFayette	111	Md.	5	1			1	3	5	C. J. F.	69 95
447	Blaney	271	Chicago	3	1				1	1	A.	15 31
448	Lincoln Park	611	do	6	1				1	2	B. C. R.	8 65
449	Clinton	26	Iowa	1					1	1	1B.	
450	Blair	393	Chicago	5	1				2	1	1H. U. S.	150 00
451	Lexington	104	do	2	1			1	1	1	A. N. Sojourner	57 38
452	Cleveland	211	do	2	1				3	5	A.	14 89
453	Harmon	17	D. C.	6	1				1	2	A. J. O.	77 33
454	Gardner	573	Ill.	3	1				1	7	C. E.	
455	Germania	182	Chicago	2	1		1				1T. U.	22 00
456	Preston	281	Ky.	1	1				1	4	A. J.	9 00
457	Mithra	410	Chicago	6	1				2	3	A.	40 55
458	Wm. R. Warren	209	do	5	1				3	17	A. J.	174 33
459	do	209	do	2	1				1	2	A. G.	18 46
460	Ashlar	308	do	5	1			1	1	5	C. J. G.	80 55
461	Arcana	274	Iowa	3	1			1	1	5	A. P.	26 90
462	Lessing	557	Chicago	3	1					2	1S. U.	
463	Germania	182	do	3	1					2	A.	38 50
464	Garden City	141	do	6	1				2	4	1B.	
465	Phœnix	96	N. Y.	1					1	2	A.	
466	T. J. Turner	409	Chicago	1	1			1	1	2	A.	23 56
467	H. W. Bigelow	438	do	5	1				3	7	A.	63 14
468	Joseph Enos	318	N. Y.	2	1				1	1	A.	4 50
469	Mithra	410	Chicago	7	1				1	3	A.	22 00
470	Garden City	141	do	2	1				1	1	A.	4 50
471	Germania	182	do	3	1				1	2	A.	15 70
472	Dearborn	310	do	3	1				1	1	A.	31 00

FINAL REPORT OF THE

No. of Application.	Lodge and No.		Location	No. in Family	Widows & Children	Provisions	Fuel	Clothing	H. Goods & Furnit'e.	Stoves	Med. Att. & Medic.	Board	Rent	Tools	Cash	Transportation	Other Aid	Insured	Letters Written	Investigations	Tickets Issued	Refused	Remarks	Total Amount Given
473	Sussex	(W. I.) 447	Kingston	6		1	1	1					2				1		1	1	2	1	D. P.	$120 37
474	Pontiac	21	Mich.	1	1															1	1	1	A.	25 00
475	Lockport	73	N. Y.	5														1	1	4	1	1	I S. V.	
476	Lincoln Park	611	Chicago	1				1											1	1	1	1	I S. U.	
477	Ark	48	N. Y.	3		1	1	1	1										1	1	5		A. P.	51 92
478	Blaney	271	Chicago	2		1	1	1	1	1							1		1	1	7	1	A.	65 35
479	Tyrian	333	Ill.	3				1	1								1	1	1	1	3		C.	18 75
480	Orient Francais	167	Mo.	4		1	1	1	1										1	2	3		C.	25 71
481	Garden City	141	Chicago	4				1	1								1	1	1	2	2		A. P.	22 28
482	Mount Hollis	192	Mass.	5				1	1								1		1	1	2		A. E.	13 19
483	Summit	192	Mich.	2		1	1	1	1								1	1	1	1	5	1	A. E.	54 81
484	Germania	182	Chicago	4													1		1	1	2	1	A.	11 00
485	Keystone	639	do	9													1		1	2	12		T. V.	134 09
486	Watertown	49	N. Y.	5	1	1	1	1	1								1		1	1	1	1	I T. V.	
487	Ashland	151	Ohio	1		1	1	1	1	1							1		1	1	5	1	A. P.	58 68
488	Mithra	410	Chicago	5		1	1	1	1								1		1	2	4		C. E.	78 94
489	Kilwinning	311	do	3		1	1	1	1	1							1		1	10	2		C. E.	86 66
490	Doric	96	England	3															1	2	7		I S. U. I.	
491	Cleveland	211	Chicago	8		1	1	1	1	1							1		1	3	13		C. E.	112 57
492	Old Well	108	Conn.	3														1	1	1	1	1	I T. U.	
493	Accordia	277	Chicago	7				1	1								1		1	2	4		A.	40 06
494	St. John's	182	Canada	2															1	1	1	1	B.	
495	Corry	365	Penn.	3															1		1	1	I S. U.	
496	Mithra	410	Chicago	3		1	1	1	1										1	1	2		A.	57 86
497	German Union	54	N. Y.	8		1	1	1	1								1		1	1	11	1	A. E.	114 03
498	Blair	393	Chicago																					

MASONIC BOARD OF RELIEF.

No.	Lodge	Location										Class	Amount
499	Non-Affiliated	Ill.		1							1	C. P.	30 00
500	Waubansia	160 Chicago	1	1							1	C. E.	59 50
501	Metropolitan	273 N. Y.	1	1							4	Sojourner, A.	25 00
502	Waubansia	160 Chicago	3			1	1				2	T. U. P.	
503	St. Croix	47 Me.	1	1							1	Sojourner, A.	36 00
504	St. Andrews	5 La.	1								2	Sojourner, A.	26 00
505	H. W. Bigelow	438 Chicago	5	1	1						2	C. E.	54 35
506	Fountain City	26 Wis.	1	1							1	A. P.	65 40
507	Blaney	271 Chicago	2	1							1	A. P.	9 50
508	Brownsville	60 Penn.	3	1				6			12	A. E.	138 87
509	Lincoln Park	611 Chicago	2	1							3	A. E.	51 61
510	Germania	182 do	6	1							5	A. E.	85 43
511	Non Affiliated	Ill.	7	1							1	S. U.	
512	St. John's	3 Conn.	1	1							2	S. U. P.	32 64
513	Kilwinning	311 Chicago	4	1							3	A.	4 60
514	Perseverance	Penn.	4	1							1	A. E. P.	37 16
515	Valley	109 N. Y.	5	1							3	A. J.	37 42
516	Lincoln Park	611 Chicago	1	1							4	A.	8 00
517	Maine	18 Me.	5	1					2	4	1	Impostor	59 95
518	Columbus	30 Ohio	9	1						1	9	A. E.	
519	Lessing	557 Chicago	4	1							1	T. U.	80 62
520	St. John's	Mass.	4	1						2	1	A.	
521	Columbus	30 Ohio	5								1	P. V.	
522	Southern Star	1158 England	2	1							1	T. U. P.	71 86
523	Union Park	610 Chicago	4	1							2	A. P.	55 29
524	Keystone	639 do	5	1							6	A. E.	110 28
525	Covenant	526 do	3	1							5	C.	33 43
526	Hesperia	411 do	1	1							110	A.	61 10
527	Kilwinning	311 do	3	1							2	A.	10 05
528	Newton	249 Ohio	2	1							6	Impostor	14 63
529	Dearborn	310 Chicago	1	1							7	A. P.	20 83
530	Germania	182 do	2	1							2	A. E.	2 60
531	Union	95 N. Y.	3	1							1	Unworthy	

130 FINAL REPORT OF THE

No. of Application.	Lodge and No.		Location.	No. in Family.	Widows & Children.	Provisions.	Fuel.	Clothing.	H. Goods & Furnit'e.	Stores.	Med. Att. & Medic.	Board.	Rent.	Tools.	Cash.	Transportation.	Other Aid.	Insured.	Letters Written.	Investigations.	Tickets Issued.	Refused.	Remarks.	Total Amount Given.
532	Fortrose	115	Scotland	4		1	1										1		1	1	5		A. P.	$41 11
533	Garden City	141	Chicago	1	1			1											1	1	2		A.	7 25
534	Greenwich	467	N. Y.	3												1			1	1			A.	66 00
535	Salem	125	Wis.	1															1	1			B.	
536	Tyrian	333	Ill.	1								1							1	1	2		A.	29 56
537	Capital	3	Neb.	1															1	1	3		Sojourner, A.	32 48
538	Not Known		N. Y.	1				1								1			1	1	4		A. E.	36 31
539	D. C. Cregier	643	Chicago	9																1	1	1	S. U.	
540	Kilwinning	311	do	5		1		1	1								1		1	1	2		A. E.	59 80
541	Humboldt	555	Ill.	4		1		1											1	1	2		T. U.	
542	Garden City	141	Chicago	1												1			1	1	2		A. P.	27 50
543	Kalamazoo	22	Mich.	6		1		1	1								1			3	10		C. E.	39 32
544	Rolling Prairie	291	Ind.	2		1		1	1	1						1			2	3	1		C. K.	127 11
545	Philadelphia	72	Penn.	1		1		1	1		1						1			1	1			Unworthy.	30 43
546	Not Known		Wis.	3		1		1									1			1	1	5	1	A. E.	
547	Mosaic	418	N. Y.	5																1	1	1		A.	69 99
548	Germania	182	Chicago	3			1	1	1											1	6		Unworthy	18 50
549	Belle City	92	Wis.	3		1		1	1								1			1	4		A. J.	48 92
550	Non-Affiliated		Ill.	1		1		1	1			1								1	5		A. E.	41 50
551	Concordia	143	N. Y.	6		1		1	1								1			1	2		Sojourner. A.	77 78
552	Springville	351	N. Y.	1																1	5		A. J. P.	19 35
553	Blaney	271	Chicago	4																1			W. T.	35 49
554	Mobile	40	Ala.	2																1			T. U.	
555	Home	508	Chicago	1																1			S. U.	
556	Dearborn	310	do	4																1	1		A. J.	32 00
557	Non-Affiliated		N. Y.	4								1								1	1			

MASONIC BOARD OF RELIEF.

No.	Name	Lodge	Location									Init.	Amount
558	Non-Affiliated		Wis.							1-2	A. E.		95 19
559	Keystone	639	Chicago					1	1	2-4	A.		85 10
560	Wm. B. Warren	209	do						1	1-6	C. G.		53 64
561	Atlas	316	N. Y.	1					1	1-1	Impostor.		
562	Kalamazoo	22	Mich.						1	1-1	T. U. P. V.		
563	Ashlar	308	Chicago					1	1	1-3	A. E.		41 52
564	Tonica	364	Ill.	1					1	2-5	A. E.		75 51
565	Port Huron	58	Mich.					1	1	1-1	A.		20 00
566	Dearborn	310	Chicago			1			1	2-1	A. J.		10 00
567	Germania	182	do						1	1-7	A.		102 44
568	Mithra	410	do						1	1-2	A.		27 93
569	do	410	do						1	1-2	A.		14 50
570	Montgomery	68	N. Y.				2		1	1	W.		
571	Fortitude	19	N. Y.	1					1	3-5	C. E.		50 15
572	Keystone	639	Chicago						1	2-5	C. p.		44 32
573	Williamson	307	Penn.						1	2-3	C. p.		44 94
574	Rising Virtue	83	Me.						1	1	S. U. P.		
575	Erie	149	Canada						1	1	S. U.		
576	Racine		Wis						1	1	S. U.		
577	Mithra	410	Chicago						1	1-2	A.		18 00
578	Wilmington	208	Ill.						1	1-4	A.		26 18
579	Union Park	610	Chicago					1	1	1	S. U.		
580	Non-Affiliated		Ohio.						1	1	S. U.		
581	Waubansia	160	Chicago						1	2-6	C. E.		47 45
582	Non-Affiliated		Ill.						1	2	S. U.		
583	Yonnondio	163	N. Y.						1	1-1	T. O.		
584	Lodi	594	Ill.						1	1-2	A. E.		18 86
585	Not Known		N. Y.	1					1	4-1	C. J.		50 00
586	Non-Affiliated		Wis.						1	4	S. U.		
587	H. W. Bigelow	438	Chicago						1	1-5	A.		60 71
588	Non-Affiliated		Quebec.						1	1-2	Sojourner. A.		11 00
589	Covenant	526	Chicago						1	1-4	A.		40 60
590	Non-Affiliated	39	Ind.						1	1-3	A.		30 99

FINAL REPORT OF THE

No. of Application	Lodge and No.	Location	No. in Family	Widows & Children	Provisions	Fuel	Clothing	B.Goods & Furnit'e	Stoves	Med. Att. & Medic.	Board	Rent	Tools	Cash	Transportation	Other Aid	Insured	Letters Written	Investigations	Tickets Issued	Refused	Remarks	Total Amount Given
591	Covenant	526 Chicago	3		1		1	1	1	1							1		1	4	1	A.	$ 49 11
592	Germania	182 do	1																2	1	1	T. U.	13 45
593	Crockett	135 Cal.	1		1	1	1								1	1	1	1	1	3		Sojourner A.	42 80
594	Champlain	237 N. Y.	4	1	1	1	1								1			1	1	3		A. J.	24 25
595	Mithra	410 Chicago	5																2	3		A. E.	
596	Belvidere	60 Ill.	2	1													1	1			1	I S. U. P.	
597	Washington	19 Ga.	3		1	1	1	1		1	1					1	1	2	2	9	1	A. E.	142 82
598	Niagara	2 Canada	1															1		2	1	T. U.	
599	Kenosha	47 Wis.	1		1		1									1	1	1	1	1		I S. U. P.	
600	Shepard	78 Conn.	2		1		1									1		1	1	2	1	A.	25 00
601	Evening Star	64 Wis.	1	1															1	1		I S. U. P.	
602	Mount Joliet	42 Ill.	2											1				1	1	1	1	S. U.	25 00
603	Covenant	526 Chicago	5							1									1		1	C. U.	
604	Milnor	132 N. Y.	3						1										1	1		I V. S.	
605	Covenant	526 Chicago	4															1	1	1		I S. U.	
606	Supreme Councils	France	2	1	1	1	1	1							1	1	1	1	1	4	6	1	A.	55 00
607	Kilwinning	311 Chicago	5	1	1	1	1	1								1		1	1	2 6		C. E.	96 44
608	do	311 do	2	1	1	1	1									1		1	1	2	2	A. E.	56 99
609	Non-Affiliated	Ind.	7											1				1	1		1	T. U.	
610	Tioga	527 N. Y.	1															1	1	2	1	A. E.	16 18
611	Erie	239 Ohio	3	1			1											1	1	1	1	B. E.	
612	Wayne	25 Ind.	2									1						1	1	2		I V. P.	27 00
613	Watertown	39 Wis.	5															1	3	1		A. E.	51 82
614	Blaney	271 Chicago	4	1	1	1	1	1							1	1	1	1	1	4		A.	73 20
615	Eastern Star	227 N. Y.	1				1		1						1	1	1	1	4		A. E.	49 62
616	Oriental	33 Chicago	4	1	1		1								1	1		1	2	2 3		A.	

MASONIC BOARD OF RELIEF. 133

No.	Lodge	Location										Amount
617	Cincinnatus	Mass.	1					1			I W.	51 99
618	Germania	182 Chicago	7	1 1			1	2	6	A.	86 52
619	St. Paul	3 Minn.	3	1 1			1	1	1	A.	100 48
620	Oriental	33 Chicago	4				1	2	1	A. E.	19 00
621	Lebanon	7 D. C.	1			1	1	1	1	Sojourner, A.	50 49
622	Battle Creek	Mich.	1	1			1	3	6	A.	90 20
623	Harmony	12 Wis.	2	1 1			1	1	4	A.	42 21
624	Wellington	127 Ohio	1	1			1	1		C. E.	
625	St. Andrews	356 Canada	6	1			3	1		I S.	84 51
626	T. J. Turner	409 Chicago	5	1			1	2		A.	
627	St. Mark's	63 Ill.	3				1			S. U. P.	9 00
628	Franklin	6 N. H.		1 1	1		2	1	4	A.	94 00
629	Union Lodge of Strict Observ.	3 Mich.	4	1				1	1	C. E.	20 00
630	Pomfret	467 England	1		1		1			Sojourner, C.	285 03
631	Blaney	271 Chicago	5	1	1		1	2	7	A. P. J. K.	7 85
632	Genesee Falls	507 N. Y.	1	1	1		2		2	Sojourner, A.	
633	Oxford	353 Penn.	2	1			1	2		I W. G.	56 16
634	Non-Affiliated	Ill.	7	1	1		1	3	2	A. J. P.	50 00
635	Blaney	271 Chicago	3	1		2		1	2	A.	43 50
636	T. J. Turner	409 do	1	1				3	3	A.	114 75
637	St. Louis B. M. R. for Chicago Masons		3								948 50
638	R. A. & K. T. Relief Com., see page 14										
639	H. W. Bigelow	438 Ohio	2	1			1	2	1	A. J. K.	50 00
640	LaFayette		2				1	1	1	Sojourner, A.	25 00
641	Worth	210 N. Y.	4	1			1	2	1	A. J.	12 65
642	Kenosha	47 Wis.	2	1			1	2	1	C. J.	50 00
643	Mount Moriah	59 La.	2	1				3	1	A. J. Sojourner	28 00
644	Non-Affiliated					1	2	1	2	A.	59 50
645	Oriental	33 Chicago	1				1			I W.	1,181 48
	Charity Account		841	6 821	4 12	1	1 1 2	10 358			30,631 37

For totals see Recapitulation V, page 134.

RECAPITULATION.

I.

Total number of applications received, ... 645
Total number of applications upon which aid was given,.......... 560
"   "   "   "   "   "   "   " refused,........ 85–645

II.

Total number of applications granted in full,.................... 395
Total number of applications granted in part, ... 88
Total number of applications granted in part, and further aid refused, because investigation showed that the party could support themselves, ... 54
Total number of applications granted in part, and further aid refused because of unworthiness,.................................. 19
Total number of applications granted in part, and further aid refused, because information was had, showing them to be impostors, ... 3
Total number of applications refused in full,.................... 85–645

III.

Total number of applications refused by action of the Full Board,.. 37
Total number of applications refused by action of the Executive Committee,... 22
Total number of applicants who declined to receive the aid offered, 11
Total number refused, for the reason that they were not vouched for, or were unable to show that they had a claim upon the Fraternity, ... 6
Total number refused, because reported "Suspended," 7
Total number refused, because reported "Expelled," 1
Total number refused, because reported "An Impostor,".......... 1—85

IV.

Of the applications made,
  Sixty-nine were from widows of M. M.'s.
  One was from the mother of a deceased M. M.
  Eight were from the daughters of M. M.'s.
  Two were from the sisters of M. M.'s.
  One was from four orphans of a M. M.
  Fourteen were from sojourning Brethren.
  One Brother, as soon as able, returned value for the full amount issued to him, and two Brethren did so in part, that the funds could be again disbursed to the needy.

V.

Total number	of applications,	645
"	" of applications from Chicago Lodges,	358
"	" of applications from other than Chicago Lodges,	202
"	" of persons represented on applications,	3,145
"	" of widows and children and female relatives of deceased M. M.'s represented,	224
"	" of persons to whom provisions was issued,	1,067
"	" of persons to whom fuel was issued,	265
"	" of persons to whom clothing was issued,	382
"	" of persons to whom household goods were issued,	291
"	" of persons to whom stoves were issued,	172
"	" of persons who received medical aid,	35
"	" of weeks' board paid for applicants,	37
"	" months' rent paid for applicants,	68
"	" of persons furnished with tools,	46
"	" to whom money was issued,	64
"	" furnished with R. R. Tickets,	189
"	" of applicants who received other relief than from this Board,	163
"	" of applicants who were insured at the time of the fire,	291
"	" of letters written on application account,	180
"	" of investigations had on application account,	1,013
"	" of orders for supplies, issued by Secretary,	3,726

VI.

At various times fifty-eight of the applicants were reported as being sick ; medical aid was offered or given in every case. Of this number, seven have died since the application was made, four of whom were buried by their several Lodges, and three at the expense of the Board.

VII.

The total amount issued to applicants, was................... $30,631 37
    Average amount issued to each applicant, $54 70.
The total amount issued to members of Chicago Lodges, was... 19,543 78
    Average amount issued to each applicant, $54 59.
The total amount issued to others than members of Chicago
    Lodges, was.. 11,087 56
    Average amount issued to each applicant, $54 84.
                                                                  $30,631 37

Largest amount issued on one application, ...$365 30
Smallest amount issued on one application, ... 1 25
    The applicants, in both cases, receiving all they asked for.

STATEMENT,

Showing the amount of supplies issued to each Chicago Lodge and Jurisdiction, and average amount given to each person.

Location of Lodge.	No. of applications.	Total am't given.	Average.
Ashlar, 308,	3	$ 70 98	$ 23 66
Apollo, 642,	1	10 95	10 95
Accordia, 277,	17	851 59	50 09
Blair, 393,	12	630 98	52 58
Blaney, 271,	12	783 69	65 30
Covenant, 526,	19	1,439 39	75 75
Chicago, 437,	7	418 78	59 82
Cleveland, 211,	13	899 83	69 22
Dearborn, 310,	9	299 34	33 26
D. C. Cregier, 643,	4	273 76	68 44
Garden City, 141,	26	585 65	22 52
Germania, 182,	70	3,951 24	56 45
H. W. Bigelow, 438,	15	845 65	56 38
Hesperia, 411,	3	267 19	89 06
Herder, 669,	1	13 50	13 50
Kilwinning, 311,	32	2,154 58	67 33
Keystone, 639,	20	1,060 46	53 02
Lessing, 557,	6	162 08	27 01
Lincoln Park, 607,	6	192 21	32 03
Mithra, 410,	35	1,606 08	45 89
National, 596,	2	147 92	73 96
Oriental, 33,	6	639 52	106 58
T. J. Turner, 409,	9	348 06	38 66
Union Park, 610,	2	85 01	42 50
Waubansia, 160,	11	761 56	69 23
W. B. Warren, 209	16	972 04	60 75
Waldeck, 674,	1	71 20	71 20
Maine,	3	100 75	33 58
New Hampshire,	1	9 00	9 00
Massachusetts,	5	155 41	31 08
Connecticut,	2	137 57	68 79
New York,	47	1,530 97	32 57
Pennsylvania,	8	408 76	51 09
Maryland,	2	74 86	37 43
Washington, D. C.,	3	54 76	18 25
South Carolina,	1	118 05	118 05
Georgia,	3	311 45	103 81
Alabama,	1	26 70	26 70
Louisiana,	2	54 00	27 00
Ohio,	5	197 21	39 44
Indiana	8	304 89	38 11
Illinois,	30	1,870 04	62 33
Kentucky,	1	22 00	22 00
Tennessee,	1	45 00	45 00
Michigan,	9	398 12	44 24

Wisconsin,	12	584 49	48 70
Minnesota,	2	123 27	61 68
Iowa,	4	220 20	55 05
Missouri,	2	114 12	57 06
Kansas,	1	63 00	63 00
Nebraska,	2	80 81	40 41
California,	4	187 73	46 93
Canada,	14	652 52	46 61
England,	5	167 14	33 43
Scotland,	4	115 03	28 76
Ireland,	3	219 97	73 32
France,	2	82 20	41 10
Germany,	1	46 21	46 21
Sweden,	2	108 06	54 03
Jamaica, W. I.,	1	120 37	120 37
Japan,	1	11 85	11 85
Non-Affiliated,	9	241 64	26 85
Commanderies and Chapters,		948 50	
Charity Account,		1,181 48	

$30,631 37

MEMORANDUM,

Of Cash returned by applicants, and received for Goods sold. The total amount is entered in the Recording Secretary's Cash Account, on page 108.

1871.
Nov. 4—From A. H. Small, for Dry Goods, etc., ...$ 7 10
  6— " Mrs. E. J. Hill, for Dry Goods, etc., ... 20 00
  29— " Wm. Peters, for Groceries, ... 35 00
1872.
Jan. 20— " W. W. Strong, for Furniture, ... 9 50
Feb. 7— " John Buckley, for Stove Pipe, ... 2 00
Mar. 6— " Chicago Relief and Aid Society, for Clothing, ... 275 00
Apr. 4— " E. N. Tucker, for Tools, ... 3 55
  11— " Knapp Pitt Works, for Tools, ... 3 25
  25— " J. E. Church, for Tools, ... 5 25
May 23— " Ed. Cook, for Tools, ... 13 46
  11— " R. H. Jordan, for Hardware, ... 35
  28— " Charles E. Hyde, for Tools, ... 18 72
  31— " J. E. Church, for Tools, ... 40
July 2— " John Felkamp, for Hardware, ... 20 25
  2— " C. Salzman, for Furniture, ... 3 00
  2— " D. J. Avery, for Safe, ... 133 00
  23— " T. T. Gurney, for Dry Goods, ... 5 35
  24— " D. C. Cregier, for Tools, ... 2 76
  24— " H. Duvall, for Furniture, ... 7 17
  24— " John Felkamp, for Desk, ... 35 00
Aug. 2— " W. A. Butters & Co., for Goods sold at Auction, .. 516 53
    " Sundry Persons, on Application Account 238 50

$1,355 14

CONCLUSION.

It is deemed proper to state that the gold drafts were sent to New York for collection, and when the returns were made the premium was credited in the aggregate. In the account of contributions of cash received, the premium on gold drafts is credited at ten and one-tenth per cent., in all cases, except where we were able to identify the draft, and credit the actual amount received, as the amount of premium received was within a fraction of that sum; but when the final statement of account was rendered by the bank, the premium on a Four Hundred Dollar gold draft, amounting to Fifty-one Dollars and fifty cents, had not been credited. This additional premium would have increased the percentage to within a slight fraction of twelve per cent. The above mentioned amount, and Seventy-seven Dollars and forty cents, a final credit by the bank for interest, is in the hands of Bro. D. C. Cregier, an acknowledgment of which will be found in the supplemental cash account, on last page of the appendix.

This record would not be complete unless the eloquent appeals to the Craft of the various Jurisdictions were made a part of it. We therefore insert, as an appendix, so far as we have been able to obtain the same, all that relates to the calls for the aid so liberally forwarded by those kind hearts who so fully realized that "it is better to give than to receive." Also, letters and extracts from letters received in acknowledgment of amounts forwarded to various Grand Jurisdictions and Lodges, as their proportion of the surplus returned.

Thus ends this glorious record—glorious in every sense, for while many gave of their abundance, others were obliged to deny themselves of their accustomed comforts to enable them to help their then well nigh despondent Brethren of Chicago. The very smallness of some of the donations received demonstrates this fact. "*Accept my mite*," was asked time and again.

Blessed Charity! First of the Heaven born, and Keystone of our Mystic Fabric.

Fraternally,

H. Duvall,
Recording Secretary.

APPENDIX.

THE ADDRESSES OF GRAND MASTERS, AND RESOLUTIONS PASSED BY VARIOUS GRAND LODGES CALLING FOR AID FOR THE FRATERNITY AT CHICAGO. ALSO LETTERS, AND EXTRACTS FROM LETTERS RECEIVED, ACKNOWLEDGING THE RECEIPT OF SURPLUS RETURNED TO GRAND JURISDICTIONS AND LODGES.

APPEAL FOR CHICAGO.

To the Worshipful Masters, Wardens, and Brethren of all Lodges of Free and Accepted Masons in the State of New York:

BRETHREN :—A calamity, one of the most appalling either of ancient or modern times, has befallen one of the fairest, and hitherto most prosperous cities of our Union. Within a brief space of time, the devastating elements has swept out of existence the public and private edifices of Chicago, destroying millions of dollars worth of property, and leaving homeless and penniless thousands of its people, among whom are many of our Brethren and their families. The cry of distress, and the prayer for relief, speedy and sufficient, reaches our ears; our hearts should not be shut to the appeal, nor our hands be idle in extending aid. We should show that our Ancient Order is founded upon Brotherly Love, and that we are ever willing to extend relief to suffering humanity.

Therefore, I. John H. Anthon, Grand Master of Masons of the State of New York, desire to lay before the Masons of the State of New York, the appeal of our suffering Brethren of Chicago, and all the desolate and oppressed of that afflicted city, in order that a fund may be raised for their immediate relief: and I do fraternally and earnestly beseech my Brethren, to give towards this object as liberally as their means will allow. I suggest contributions in money, knowing that Relief Committees will be organized, and that such sums as may be raised will be disbursed by them in a proper and efficient manner. Contributions sent in drafts on New York, to the order of the Grand Master, at his office, No. 271, Broadway, will be by him forwarded to Chicago.

J. H. ANTHON.

Grand Master's Office, New York, Oct. 9, 1871.

140 FINAL REPORT OF THE

GRAND LODGE OF MASSACHUSETTS.

BOSTON, October 10, 1871.

To the Master, Wardens and Brethren of our several Lodges :

The terrible conflagration at Chicago, has thrown our Brethren there into great need and suffering. They require the moneys of the Craft to give them food, clothing and shelter. Upon receipt of this, please collect by subscription from the members of your Lodge, or vote from your funds such an amount as you can, consistently, and forthwith forward it to our Grand Secretary, Charles H. Titus, Masonic Temple, Boston, by whom it will be forwarded to our suffering, houseless, destitute Brethren in Chicago. Let Massachusetts not be behind in this great work of Charity.

" Do good unto all, but more especially unto those of the household of the faithful." Fraternally,
WILLIAM S. GARDNER,
Grand Master.

GRAND LODGE OF CONNECTICUT.

OFFICE OF THE GRAND MASTER.
BRIDGEPORT, Conn., Oct. 11, A. L. 5871.

To the Masons of Connecticut :

The awful calamity which has befallen our Brethren in Chicago, calls upon the Fraternity for the prompt and generous exercise of our Masonic Charity, that relief may be extended at once to our homeless Brethren, and their starving families. I, therefore, fraternally and earnestly, call upon our Lodges and individual Masons, to contribute to this end as promptly and liberally as their means will allow. Let each Lodge, at its first meeting, therefore, donate such sums as they can. Contributions, sent in checks or drafts, to the order of the Grand Master, at Bridgeport, will be promptly acknowledged, and sent to Chicago, to our R. W. Representative near the M. W. Grand Lodge of Illinois.

Fraternally Yours,
JAMES L. GOULD, *Grand Master.*
Attest : J. K. WHEELER, *Grand Secretary.*

OFFICE OF THE GRAND MASTER OF ANCIENT FREE AND ACCEPTED MASONS OF THE STATE OF NEW JERSEY.

TENAFLY, October 10th, 1871.

To the Worshipful Master, Wardens and Brethren of .... Lodge, No..

BRETHREN :—A calamity unparalleled in the annals of our country, has befallen one of the most flourishing cities of the West. In a single day thousands of families in the city of Chicago have been rendered homeless and houseless, and are now without food. Their destitute condition appeals to all for sympathy and aid.

The mission of Masonry is the relief of want and woe, and never before have we had so great an opportunity to demonstrate its teachings by our acts.

Therefore, I, Wm. E. Pine, Grand Master of Masons of the State of New Jersey, fraternally appeal to your sympathies for aid in behalf of our suffering Brethren and their families in that afflicted city.

Contributions in money or draft, sent to Bro. Jos. H. Hough, Grand Secretary, at Trenton, subject to my order, will be forwarded without delay, to M. W. Dewitt C. Cregier, Grand Master of Masons of Illinois, to be distributed as his good judgment may dictate.

Fraternally,
WILLIAM E. PINE, *Grand Master.*
Attest: Jos. H. HOUGH, *Grand Secretary.*

GRAND LODGE OF PENNSYLVANIA, F. AND A. M.

EXTRA GRAND COMMUNICATION,
Held at Philadelphia, October 22, A D. 1871, A. L. 5871.

P. G. M. Brother James Page offered the following, which was adopted, viz:

WHEREAS, The City of Chicago has been overtaken by a dreadful and appalling calamity, by which it has been reduced almost to a waste of burning ruins, and its people, to a large extent rendered houseless and homeless, and thousands of them are now suffering for want of food and clothing:

Therefore, be it Resolved, That this Grand Lodge do at once contribute in aid of the afflicted of this terribly smitten city, the sum of One Thousand Dollars, the same to be remitted to the M. W. the Grand Master of the Grand Lodge of Illinois, at Chicago, to be by him distributed to and among our suffering Brethren there, as to him shall seem to be most wise and judicious.

Resolved, That this Grand Lodge earnestly recommends to all the subordinate Lodges within her jurisdiction, the propriety of contributing immediately, to the best of their respective abilities, in aid of their suffering Brethren in Chicago, and that all sums of money set apart by them for such purpose, be placed at the disposal of the R. W. Grand Master, to be by him in like manner remitted to the M. W. the Grand Master of the Grand Lodge of Illinois, at Chicago.

Resolved, That a special Committee of Seven, be appointed to appeal to the several Lodges in the State in furtherance of the object of these resolutions.

Extract from the minutes.

JOHN THOMSON, *Grand Secretary.*

The R. W. Grand Master was pleased to appoint the following named Brethren as the Committee alluded to above:

Past Grand Master Brother James Page, of Lodge No. 126.
Brother E. Harper Jeffries,   "   "   186.
    "   Charles D. Freeman,   "   "   130.
    "   Conrad B. Day,   "   "   52.
    "   Alfred Slack,   "   "   318.
    "   James M. Porter,   "   "   152.
    "   William Himrod, Jr.,   "   "   362.

W. M., Officers and Brethren of Lodge No. _____

We fraternally call your attention to the foregoing preamble and resolutions of the Grand Lodge, adopted at a Special G. C., on the evening of the 12th September, 1871, and invoke in the name of Brotherly-Love and Masonic Charity, your early, cordial and prompt action in the premises.

A terrible calamity has befallen the people of Chicago. The almost entire destruction by fire of their once prosperous and beautiful city, is an event that causes every bosom to thrill with sorrow, and sends its appeal to every humane heart. The desolation which has overwhelmed that enterprising community, is without a parallel in the history of this country, and in its extent, without comparison in modern times. The wailing cry from the houseless, the homeless, the destitute, the sick and the suffering, is heard throughout our land. They need shelter, they need raiment, they need food. Shall Masonry in our Jurisdiction close its ears to their touching and heart-rending cry for help? We know it will not, but that the Grand Lodge doing all that she can in view of her present financial condition, and appealing to her children, will be cheerfully and promptly aided by them, in her effort to grant relief and impart consolation to our suffering Brethren in the City of the Lake, in this the hour of their desolation and sorrow.

"And now abideth Faith, Hope and Charity, these three, but the greatest of these is Charity."

           Affectionately and Fraternally,

                          JAMES PAGE,
                          E. HARPER JEFFRIES,
                          CHAS. D. FREEMAN,
        Committee,   CONRAD B. DAY,
                          ALFRED SLACK,
                          JAS. M. PORTER,
                          WM. HIMROD, Jr.,

OFFICE OF THE R. W GRAND MASTER OF F. AND A. M. OF PENNSYLVANIA.

                  MASONIC HALL, PHILADELPHIA, Oct. 13, 1871.

It is requested that all contributions made by the Lodges be forwarded to the R. W. Grand Secretary, John Thomson, Masonic Hall, Philadelphia, who will acknowledge their receipt, and transmit them as the donations of the respective Lodges to the M. W. Grand Master of Illinois, to be disbursed, under his direction, for the relief of our suffering Brethren in Chicago.

                     R. A. LAMBERTON, *Grand Master.*

GRAND LODGE OF THE DISTRICT OF COLUMBIA.

[Extract from Grand Master Chas. F. Stansbury's Address.]

* * * On the 8th and 9th of October, an appalling calamity which has stirred the sympathy of the whole world, befell the great city of Chicago, in the destruction of its fairest and richest portion by fire. You are all familiar with the facts, as they have been given to the public by the press ; but no description can convey an adequate impression of the vast extent and awful character and effects of the conflagration. Among the sufferers were many of our Brethren, who, as individuals, had their homes and places of business swept away ; and, as Masons, shared in the common destruction of their Lodge rooms and other places of assembly, and of all the precious archives and relics which were gathered in them.

When the news reached our city I immediately called a mass meeting of the Fraternity, which was held in the Temple, on the evening of October 11th. Fifteen Hundred Dollars were paid in on that occasion for the relief of our suffering Brethren ; and the sum was subsequently increased to $2,868 40, which was conveyed by a special committee to Chicago, and handed over to the Grand Master of Masons of Illinois. The committee was received with the greatest courtesy and kindness by the Grand Master and other Brethren of Chicago, who accepted our contribution with every expression of appreciation of the promptitude with which it was offered, and the fraternal feeling in which it had its motive. Since the return of the Committee a further sum has been collected, which, it is expected, will be considerably increased by the proceeds of the Concert to be given on the 16th inst., by the Masonic Choir, for the benefit of the same benevolent object.

Our thanks are due to Hon. John W. Garrett, President of the Baltimore & Ohio Railroad, and to D. W. Caldwell, Superintendent of the Road from Columbus to Chicago, for their liberality and courtesy in providing free transportation for our offerings, and passes to and from Chicago for the members of our Relief Committee. * * *

GRAND LODGE OF KENTUCKY.

[Extract from the Grand Master's Address.]

* * * " The Home erected by Kentucky liberality, as a Home for the homeless widows and orphans of deceased Kentucky Masons, and those in charge thereof, without violating the trust confided to them, enabled Kentucky, through Past Grand Master Charles Tilden, and Brothers T. L. Jefferson, C. Henry Finck and A. H. Gardner, to be the first to offer a temporary home to the suffering women and children of desolate Chicago.

That committee, from personal investigation, ascertained that eighteen Blue Lodges, two Commanderies, all the Scottish Rite and Chapter rooms of that city, had been destroyed by the fire fiend, and our afflicted Brethren realized that there was something in Masonry, when a committee from a distant State came and said ; " Give us your women and children, and we will take them to a home where they will have a brother's care, until you are again severally in possession of happy homes of your own."

There is a reasonable probability of that offer being accepted ; and if it is, I know the Masonic heart too well to doubt its being sacredly fulfilled.

And to the end that this Grand Lodge may do its part towards this great benificence, I recommend that a specific sum be appropriated from our Treasury to be used in extending the proper relief." * * *

GRAND MASTER'S OFFICE, GRAND LODGE OF THE STATE OF LOUISIANA, FREE AND ACCEPTED MASONS.

NEW ORLEANS, October 16th, 1871.

To the W. M., Officers and Members of .... Lodge No....

BRETHREN :—A heavy calamity has fallen upon the city of Chicago ; an immense number of its inhabitants have been deprived of their property, and rendered homeless and destitute by the terrible fire which has almost destroyed their late flourishing and beautiful city.

The people of our land, also of the old world, have promptly responded to the cry for assistance ; food, clothing and money has been liberally given to supply the immediate pressing wants of the sufferers, and in this noble benevolence our Fraternity have not been behind their fellow citizens ; but we, as Masons, have a duty to perform toward our own Brethren in that stricken city. In addition to this, extensive conflagrations have occurred in Michigan and other States of the Northwest—property and life have been sacrificed ; whole sections of country laid waste, and the severity of a Northern winter awaits the unfortunate survivors. I therefore call upon the Lodges and Masons of Louisiana to contribute from their means in aid of our Brethren, many thousands of whom are, with their families, among the sufferers. Let us promptly show our sympathy with the suffering members of that Fraternity who in the darkest hours of trouble and misfortune never fail to respond freely to calls for fraternal aid.

SAM'L M. TODD, *Grand Master.*

GRAND LODGE OF MISSOURI.

RELIEF FOR CHICAGO.

[Extract from the Grand Master's Address.]

The most terrible of all destroyers has just accomplished his master-piece in the world's history, and chose for his field a sister city in our neighboring Jurisdiction of Illinois. The fire-king has swept a great metropolis out of existence, and made houseless and homeless two hundred thousand people. Chicago is a story of yesterday. Little or nothing is left of one of the wonders of our Continent, but a vast waste of coals and ashes, and a quarter of a million of suffering people, who lived in or depended upon the doomed city for support. The jaws of an earthquake never opened and closed with such crushing effect upon the lives and substance of men, as the habitations and fortunes of our Brethren of Chicago have been swallowed up by this dire calamity. I have no words to express what I feel in this connection, and what I know must be the sense of the Grand Lodge of Missouri. Let us not give play to our feelings but in action. The misfortunes and needs of so large a mass of humanity appeal, not alone to our charity as Masons, but to our manhood. Let us do all we can do promptly, and, while we lament the necessity, be proud of our condition to respond to the cry for sympathy and aid. Chicago was of wood. What we give now will contribute to rebuild the city of more enduring marble. I recommend the referrence of the matter to a special committee, with instructions to act at once.

OFFICE OF THE GRAND HIGH PRIEST OF ROYAL ARCH MASONS IN IOWA.

DUBUQUE, October 24, 1871.

To the M. E. H. P., King, Scribe and Companions of ------ Chapter No.__ :

COMPANIONS :—The recent direful calamity which visited Chicago, destroyed a large number of Masonic altars, and rendered homeless many hundreds of our Brethren. They appeal for aid to the Craft. Universal and nobly is that appeal being responded to, not only in America, but also abroad. Iowa should not be in the rear in this movement. Already the Grand Chapter has given Two Hundred Dollars to our suffering frators. Will not the Chapters, all and singular, likewise heed the cry of the needy? I suggest that each Chapter make a donation of at least $5, forwarding that, or a larger sum to me, and I will see that it is promptly remitted to the M. W. Grand Master of Masons in Illinois, Brother Dewitt C. Cregier ; or if the contributors prefer, they may at once address that distinguished Grand Officer. " If it were done, when 't is done, then 't were well it were done quickly ;" therefore, do I urge it upon you, Companions, to give this matter immediate attention.

EDWARD A. GUILBERT, *Grand High Priest.*

OFFICE OF GRAND SECRETARY, GRAND LODGE OF KANSAS.

LEAVENWORTH, October 27, 1871.

DEAR SIR AND BROTHERS :—In compliance with the order of the M. W. Grand Lodge of Kansas, I hasten to lay before your Lodge, for its immediate consideration, the following resolutions, which were adopted at our last Annual Communication, held on the 19th instant, to-wit:

Resolved, That this M. W. G. Lodge of A. F. and A. M. of Kansas, in Annual Convention, and in behalf of their Brethren under this Masonic Jurisdiction, extend to the Brethren in Chicago their profound sympathy in the affliction and distress they are called upon to endure in consequence of the recent great fire in that city.

Resolved, That the sum of Five Hundred Dollars be, and the same is hereby appropriated from the General Fund of this Grand Lodge, for the relief of our Chicago Brethren.

Resolved, That in addition to the foregoing appropriation, this Grand Lodge earnestly recommend to the subordinate Lodges of this State, to liberally contribute for the relief of our Chicago Brethren ; and further recommend that such contributions should aggregate an amount in dollars equal at' least to the membership of the Order in this State.

Resolved, That the contributions from the subordinate Lodges, contemplated in the foregoing resolution, shall be transmitted, by the proper Officers of each Lodge, to the M. W. Grand Master of this Jurisdiction, who shall forward the same, together with the Five Hundred Dollars appropriated under the foregoing second resolution, to the M. W. Grand Master of the State of Illinois, the whole to be by him disbursed in such a manner as he may deem best to relieve the sufferings of our Chicago Brethren, and, in his judgement, will best subserve the wishes and intentions of this Grand Lodge.

You will advise the M. W. Grand Master, John M. Price, of Atchison, Kansas, of your action at as early a day as possible.

Yours, Fraternally,

JOHN H. BROWN, *Grand Secretary.*

FROM THE EAST OF THE M. W. GRAND LODGE OF THE STATE OF ILLINOIS, A. F. AND A. M.

To the Masters, Wardens and Brethren of the Constituent Lodges, Greeting :

In the life-time of institutions, as of men, there comes supreme moments to put their value to the proof ; to test their moral fibre, and sift their claims to the world's regard.   In such an hour not what we *profess*, but what we *are* and what we *do* must vindicate our fitness to exist.

Such an hour comes to Masonry now, through one of the most appalling calamities of all time: and now or never she must prove her birthright by her care for her stricken children. The tree is to be judged by its fruit. The emergency that is now upon us is to determine whether our suffering Brethren, whose wail of distress sighs in every breeze that sweeps over the ashes of Chicago, shall have cause, when they look back upon the winter of privations which followed that hideous nightmare of October, to nurse the bitter reflection that they leaned upon a broken reed, or whether they shall recur to it with grateful memories of Masonic charity walking with transfigured and pitying feet amid the embers of their ruined homes, sheltering their little ones beneath the wings of her compassion, and dropping relief from her open hands.

It is to determine, too, whether the vows of benevolence which we have assumed at the altar of Masonry have been of the lips only, or of the heart; whether the influence of her holy teachings has stirred only that superficial level where the mere *sentiment* of brotherhood flares its brief moment, or has struck deeper and kindled into an enduring glow the love which manifests itself in deeds. If Masonry has indeed taken hold upon our hearts, in each one of them will be heard the echo of the still small voice which from within the *Sanctum Sanctorum* repeats the oft-uttered admonition, "Give to your distressed Brother as his necessities require and your abilities permit."

Brethren! The necessities of our suffering fellows in Chicago are without limit. Until we have exhausted our ability to give, a sacred duty remains unfulfilled. Already many of you have done nobly; your unasked charity, like that of others throughout the land, coming on swift wings to the rescue. While yet a whole city lay stunned and bewildered, echoing footsteps of the almoners of your bounty awakened hope in the bosoms of the down-stricken and despairing. Blessings on their unknown benefactors fell from the lips of famishing children, and eyes long unused to weeping were wet with thankful tears.

Careful, self-sacrificing men, still husband your contributions and prudently apply them to the relief of the most destitute. But the long winter is before them, and with it will come that steady drain upon their resources which only your best efforts can repair.

Let every craftsman, then, give to the utmost of his ability, and learn anew the lesson; "It is more blessed to give than to receive." God help us all to do our duty. We suggest no definite plan, except that in some systematic way the needs and duty of the hour should be brought home to every Mason. How they shall be reached, and with the best results, we leave to the judgment of each particular Lodge. Whatever the diversity of plan in different localities, we confidently look for such a unity of purpose and such energy in its pursuit that the result of your efforts shall be commensurate with the awful necessity.

Let your contributions be forwarded to the Grand Master, at the Water Works, Chicago: they will be duly acknowledged and recorded.

DEWITT C. CREGIER, G. M.,
JAMES A. HAWLEY, D. G. M.,
GEO. E. LOUNSBURY, S. G. W.,
JOSEPH ROBBINS, J. G. W.,
HARRISON DILLS, G. Treas.

Given this 29th day of November, A. D. 1871, A. L. 5871.

ORLIN H. MINER, *Grand Secretary.*

LETTERS ACKNOWLEDGING RECEIPT OF SURPLUS RETURNED.

OFFICE OF THE GRAND MASTER OF MASONS OF THE STATE OF MAINE.

AUGUSTA, September 23d, 1872.

M. W. D. C. Cregier, Grand Master of Illinois:

DEAR SIR AND BROTHER:—Yours of August 24th, has just reached me. With this please find receipt for One Hundred and Twelve Dollars, sent from you to our Grand Lodge.

It is with devout gratitude to our Supreme Grand Master, that he moved the hearts of the Fraternity to contribute to the relief of our suffering Brethren in your city so that a surplus has been returned.

Please excuse haste, and accept this from a Brother who would be glad to greet you in Maine. Fraternally Yours,

DAVID CARGILL,
Grand Master of Masons in Maine.

GRAND LODGE OF MASSACHUSETTS.

MASONIC TEMPLE, BOSTON, Sept. 21, 1872.

D. C. Cregier, Esq., Grand Master, etc.

DEAR SIR AND M. W. BROTHER:—Please find inclosed the receipt of our Grand Treasurer for the amount returned to us from the donations made from our Jurisdiction.

We rejoice that you find your necessities met by the liberality of your Brethren, and we accept the surplus returned, with a grateful appreciation of that nice sense of honor that causes its return to us, and shall sacredly devote it to the cause of Masonic charity.

Most Truly and Fraternally Yours,

CHARLES H. TITUS, Grand Secretary.

OFFICE OF THE GRAND MASTER OF MASONS, OF CONNECTICUT.

GREENWICH, CONN., Sept. 16, A. L. 5872.

M. W. Dewitt C. Cregier, Grand Master of Masons of Illinois:

MY DEAR SIR AND M. W. BROTHER:—Your favor of August 24th, 1872, came to hand this morning, enclosing draft on New York for $332 00, being the surplus of the funds contributed by the Brethren of Connecticut, over and above the amount necessary for the relief of our Brethren of Illinois, under their yet recent severe affliction.

I am wholly unable to express the emotions caused by the perusal of your truly fraternal letter. Surprise and delight were mingled ; surprise at the receipt of the most unexpected enclosure, and delight that the grievous necessities of our Chicago Brethren had been abundantly relieved, and, above all, that our Illinois Brethren had displayed to the World, in these degenerate days, a bright example of the most delicate and refined sense of the highest Honor.

The Masons of Connecticut, from the overflow of their hearts, contributed most gladly of their substance, scarcely daring to hope that the necessities of their Brethren could be relieved, much less, that a portion of their charity would be returned.

It seems to me, M. W. Brother, that your suggestion of placing this return in the "Charity Fund" of our Grand Lodge, is the only proper disposition which could be made of it. Consecrated as the heart offering of the Masons of Connecticut, upon the blessed Altar of Charity, and returned to their sacred keeping, from the abundance of that Altar, it should remain at its Shrine, set apart for the beneficent purposes of that which is the Bond of Peace, the Perfection of every virtue, extending beyond the grave, into the boundless realms of Eternity.

Accept our thanks for the judicious and most acceptable manner in which you and your associates of the Masonic Board of Relief have performed their arduous duties in this behalf.

The Grand Lodge of Connecticut will, at its next annual communication, make suitable acknowledgment of your noble conduct, and a proper disposition of the funds you have so unexpectedly placed in its hands.

With assurance of the highest respect and esteem, and with most earnest Fraternal greetings, I remain,

Very Truly and Fraternally Yours,

L. A. LOCKWOOD, Grand Master.

OFFICE OF THE GRAND MASTER OF MASONS IN THE STATE OF NEW YORK.

BUFFALO, Sept. 14, 1872.

Dewitt C. Creyier, Esq., Grand Master of Masons in the State of Illinois :

M. W. SIR AND DEAR BROTHER :—I have the honor to acknowledge the receipt of your letter dated Aug. 24, ult., enclosing draft on New York for $3,404.17, being the amount awarded by the late Board of Masonic Relief of the city of Chicago, to the Grand Lodge of New York, from the surplus of funds contributed by the Fraternity to aid the Brethren of Chicago, who were rendered destitute by reason of the great conflagration which visited that city in October last, and which you desire should be appropriated to our "Hall and Asylum Fund," or applied to such other use as the Grand Lodge may direct.

In compliance with your wish, the money will be paid to the Treasurer of that fund, subject to further direction of the Grand Lodge, at its annual meeting, in June of next year.

The Masons of this Jurisdiction had no wish or expectation that any of the funds contributed by them should be returned, and they will recognize in this case an integrity on the part of the Masons of Chicago, which honors the teachings of the Craft.

I accept this noble contribution to the "Masonic Hall and Asylum Fund" of our Jurisdiction, which comes from the Masons of Chicago; and I desire, through you, M. W. Sir, to express the hearty thanks of the Grand Lodge of New York, for the liberal donation, and the sincere wish that Masons everywhere may be as just, liberal and generous as their Brethren of Chicago.

I am, M. W. Sir, truly and Fraternally, your Friend and Brother,
CHRISTOPHER G. FOX, G. M.

OFFICE OF THE GRAND MASTER OF ANCIENT FREE AND ACCEPTED MASONS OF THE STATE OF NEW JERSEY.

NEWARK, September 16, 1872.
Hon. Dewitt C. Cregier, Grand Master of Masons in Illinois:

M. W. SIR AND BROTHER :—Your favor, enclosing draft on New York, bearing date 11th inst., for One Thousand and Eighty Dollars, the *pro rata* amount of surplus funds remaining on hand at the close of the labors of the Masonic Board of Relief of your Jurisdiction, is at hand.

I am glad to know the wants of our Brethren, made needy by the conflagration of October last, have been supplied; and be assured, my dear Brother, the zeal and fidelity with which the Masonic Board of Relief of Chicago has discharged its onerous duties, is most gratefully appreciated by the Craft of New Jersey.

I herewith return receipt, as requested, and have the honor to remain,
Faithfully and Fraternally Yours,
WM. E. PINE, Grand Master.

OFFICE OF THE R. W., THE GRAND MASTER OF FREE AND ACCEPTED MASONS OF PENNSYLVANIA.

MASONIC HALL, PHILADELPHIA, Sept. 23, 1872.
M. W. Dewitt C. Cregier, Grand Master of Masons of Illinois:

M. W. SIR AND BROTHER :—I take the earliest opportunity, after my return from the pleasing mission to which your courtesy requested my attention, in the examination of the proceedings of the Masonic Board of Relief for sufferers by the great fire at Chicago, to acknowledge your letter of Aug. 24, inclosing check to my order, of Two Thousand One Hundred and Fifty 40-100 Dollars, ($2,150 40,) proportion of surplus of Relief Fund returned to the Grand Lodge of Pennsylvania. I feel sure, M. W. Sir and Brother, that the Grand Lodge of Pennsylvania, and her subordinate Lodges, had no thought, when they freely and most cheerfully contributed to the Relief Fund, of a return of any portion of their gifts. And while, in common with our Brethren in sister Jurisdictions, we are gratified to learn that the total amount contributed more than sufficed, under judicious management and disbursement, for the purposes intended; we unite with what must be the universal voice of the Fraternity, in bearing testimony to the nice sense of honor, and innate delicacy of feeling, which has prompted the return of the surplus. The action of the Board of Relief in this regard cannot fail to meet the entire approbation of the Craft.

It is an encouragement to the exercise of a free and spontaneous charity, thus to find what, indeed, from the noble precepts of our Fraternity, was only to be expected such scrupulous and exact regard for high principles.

The funds have been placed in the hands of the Grand Treasurer, and the matter will be reported to the Grand Lodge, at the next Grand Communication, that such action may be taken for their disposition as may be deemed most in accordance with the circumstances of their return.

With grateful recollections of the many courtesies extended by yourself and the Brethren of Chicago during my recent visit, I remain,
Very Truly and Fraternally Yours,
SAM'L C. PERKINS, Grand Master.

NEWTOWN, CONN., Sept. 24th, 1872.
D. C. Cregier, Esq., Grand Master of Masons in Illinois:

M. W. SIR AND BROTHER:—Your communication, under date of 24th of August, enclosing check upon the Metropolitan National Bank, New York, for One Hundred Dollars, being sum returned through you to the Masons of La., by the Masonic Board of Relief, of Chicago, has been forwarded to me, at this place, and I have, as requested, signed the receipt for the amount, and enclose the same herewith.

I am much pleased to find that the Brethren in Chicago, having sufficient for the wants of the needy in their midst, have so large a surplus, which can be bestowed upon Brethren elsewhere.

I propose, with the consent of the original donors of the sum sent from Louisiana, to place the amount returned by you, in the hands of Louisiana Relief Lodge, No. 1, New Orleans, which body has had, during the past year many calls upon it for relief of sojourning Brethren and their families.

Fraternally Yours, SAM'L M. TODD,
Grand Master of Masons in Louisiana.

THE GRAND LODGE OF IOWA, A. F. & A. M.

OFFICE OF THE GRAND MASTER,
MUSCATINE, Sept. 28, A. D. 1872.

Hon. D. C. Cregier, Grand Master:

DEAR SIR AND M. W. BROTHER:—I have the honor to acknowledge the receipt of your esteemed favor of August 24th, covering your draft for the sum of $204 00, to the credit of the Grand Lodge of Iowa, as the estimated amount of the sum contributed by the Lodges of this Jurisdiction, for the relief of the distressed Brethren of your city, yet remaining unexpended, and above the wants of those for whose benefit it was advanced.

I am unable, my dear Brother, to express to you the surprise and pleasure which your letter, and the examination I have been permitted to make of the books of your "Masonic Board of Relief," has afforded me. In these I find evidences of the most thorough and scrupulous care in the management and distribution of the large sums which the Craft furnished you, and at the same time not less convincing evidence that no deserving case was allowed to go unrelieved.

The large sum which you have so unexpectedly returned to the contributing Bodies, is proof of the fact that the history of no other organization excels our own in that practical exemplification of charity which, while it prevents imposition, the giver supplies all the actual wants of the needy, and yet does not take from him either the capacity or the disposition to assist himself.

The work which the "Board of Relief" has accomplished, under your guidance, the singularly clear and methodical manner in which the detailed records of how the moneys received have been expended, the skill and wisdom which have attended the efforts of the Board, and, above all, the conspicuous unselfishness and integrity which have marked its entire action, constitute the brightest page in the history of our Order, and of that most wonderful of all events, the Chicago fire.

It has been often remarked that no evil, great or small, can occur without its compensating good. The history of the "Masonic Board of Relief," of Chicago, comprising, as it does, on the one hand, the spontaneous and fraternal outpouring of Masonic generosity, and on the other the careful, painstaking and honorable distribution of this generosity by the Board, makes up no small portion of the compensating good that followed the great disaster. They showed to the world that in ministering to distress, Masons stopped not to count their gifts; and in the darkest hour the recipients allowed no feelings of personal loss to swerve them from the strictest path of Masonic honesty. History can show no brighter page anywhere.

With best wishes for yourself and Masons of Chicago, I am

Truly and Fraternally Yours,

O. P. WATERS, Grand Master in Iowa.

OFFICE OF GRAND MASTER, GRAND LODGE, A. F. & A. M.,
STATE OF MISSOURI.

St. Louis, September 13th, 1872.

D. C. Cregier, Esq., Chicago, Ill., Grand Master of Masons:

DEAR SIR AND M. W. BROTHER :—Your letter, enclosing draft, etc., reached me to-day. I am certain that none of the contributors of our $1,150 to the "Chicago Relief Fund" ever expected a return of any of the money. Your act of generosity,—I can call it nothing else, it is more than justice,—will be a great surprise to our Grand Lodge. On its behalf I can only thank you, and other members of your Board of Relief. Such episodes as this increase confidence in each other, and make Masonic bonds stronger. They also teach a public lesson which does justice to the principles which we profess, and the motives by which we claim to be guided. Enclosed you will find receipt, as per request.

With admiration for the kind of material of which Chicago Masons are made, I am, Very Truly and Fraternally,

THOS. E. GARRETT, Grand Master of Missouri.

OFFICE OF THE GRAND MASTER OF THE GRAND LODGE OF NEBRASKA, A. F. & A. M.

NEBRASKA CITY, Sept. 15, 1872.

M. W. D. C. Cregier, Grand Master, Ill.:

MOST WORSHIPFUL SIR AND BROTHER :—Your communication, enclosing draft on New York for One Hundred and Fourteen Dollars, is received. I have placed the money in bank, subject to the disposal of our next Grand Lodge. Your action should, and I have no doubt will, receive the highest commendation from the various Grand Lodges. It certainly commends itself to all well disposed and well thinking men. May the applause of the Brethren throughout the world be your reward. I have the honor to be,

Truly and Fraternally Yours,

W. E. HILL, Grand Master of Nebraska.

GRAND LODGE OF CANADA.

OFFICE OF THE GRAND MASTER,
SIMCOE, ONT., Sept. 16, 1872.

MOST WORSHIPFUL SIR AND DEAR BROTHER :—I hasten to acknowledge the receipt of your letter, dated 24th of August, covering a draft on New York for $994 20, being the share, *pro rata*, of unexpended funds contributed by the Masons of Canada, in aid of the fund raised for the relief of those Masons who suffered from the great fire at Chicago, in October last, and I now enclose you the receipt of our Grand Treasurer for that amount

I most heartily approve of the decision of your Committee, in returning funds not required for the purposes for which they were contributed, and their action in this matter will hereafter be cited as a noble precedent for our guidance in all time to come.

This money is now placed to the credit of our Grand Lodge, and that amount, and every dollar in our treasury, is at all times available in response to the call of suffering humanity, and as an exemplification of our appreciation of the great cardinal virtues of Brotherly-love—Relief and Truth.

I continue, Most Worshipful Sir and Dear Brother,

Very Truly and Fraternally Yours,

WM. M. WILSON, Grand Master, G. L. C.

To the M. W. Bro. DEWITT C. CREGIER, Esq., Grand Master of Masons of Illinois, and late President of the Masonic Board of Relief, Chicago.

NEW YORK, October 19th, 1872.

M. W. SIR AND BROTHER:—In acknowledging the receipt of your very kind and fraternal favor, of the 9th ult., it becomes my pleasing duty to inform you that, at a regular communication of Independent Royal Arch Lodge, No. 2, F. A. M., held on the 3d inst., it was unanimously

Resolved, That this Lodge acknowledge, with sincere admiration, the noble generosity of the Board of Relief of Chicago, in the return of the unexpended balance of the funds committed to its charge. It is further

Resolved, That the warm thanks of this Lodge be, and they are hereby tendered the M. W. Grand Master of the Grand Lodge of Illinois, for the kind terms in which he recognizes the contributions of the Masons of New York, which certainly was the mere discharge of an evident Masonic duty.

Very Truly and Fraternally Yours,

HENRY D. WALKER, Master.

Attest: GEO. PERAULT, Secretary.

To DEWITT C. CREGIER, Esq., Grand Master of Masons, Illinois, Chicago.

EXTRACTS.

[From Hon. Alex. H. Newcomb. Grand Master of Ohio.]

* * * It is very gratifying to know that you had enough to meet the wants of those who, by the great fire of October last, needed your assistance. * * *

[From Hon. Wm. A. Von Bokkeleo, Grand Master of Nevada.]
* * * We acknowledge the receipt of the draft, with great pleasure, as it is an evidence that the contributions of the craft were, as they should always be, in excess of, rather than less than the necessity of the occasion ; and that, as dispensers of our assistance, due attention has been paid that no waste be allowed. * * *

[From Hop. Edward A. Guilbert, Grand High Priest of Iowa.]
* * * I congratulate you on the success of your Relief endeavor, and recommend your final disposition of the surplus. * * *

[From Seth E. Marsh, W. M. of St. John's Lodge, No. 4, of Hartford, Conn.]
* * * Be assured that the Officers and Brethren of St. John's Lodge, No. 4, will appreciate the motives, and principles of right and justice, which have actuated your Honorable Board, and consider them a thousand times more valuable than the amount returned. * * *

[From Geo. W. Tuller, W. M., of Hartford Lodge, No. 88, Conn.]
* * * Have no doubt but that the Lodge will feel that Masonry in Chicago is what it should be throughout the world. * * *

[From C. H. Rogers, Secretary of Plymouth Lodge, Mass.]
* * * Voted that the amount returned be accepted in the spirit which prompted its return, and that the thanks of the Lodge be tendered you for the same. * * *

[From Cornelius Glen, Secretary of Masters Lodge, No. 5, Albany, N. Y.]
* * * The members of our Lodge are perfectly satisfied with the manner in which the charge committed to you has been fulfilled, and it is a source of pleasure to know that after relieving all, there was more than sufficient, and hence a return made. * * *

[From J. B. White, W. M. of Holland Lodge, No. 8, New York.]
* * * Permit me to assure you of the pleasure with which we were enabled to afford any assistance to our needy Brethren on that occasion, and the gratification with which we learn of their returning prosperity, as evinced in your very honorable action in this matter. * * *

[From Nevin W. Butler, Secretary of Montauk Lodge, No. 286, Brooklyn, N. Y.]
* * * We surely can have no better evidence than this fact, that the trust imposed upon that Board has been most faithfully and judiciously discharged ; and we trust that upon all future occasions, when the cry of distress shall come up from our Masonic Brethren, wherever they may be, the great tenets of our profession may be as faithfully carried out by those whose privilege it will be to contribute, as by those whose task it may be to distribute. Such display of the grand principles of Masonry cannot but result in good, and must compel the admiration of the world, and the admission that Masonry is more than an empty name. * * *

[From Edmund P. Fox, W. M., of Gloversville Lodge, No. 429, N. Y.]
* * * We do so only in the true fraternal spirit in which it is returned, and that in this action of your Board of Relief, we fully recognize an eminent exemplification of the principles of Masonic charity and benevolence.

[From Haynes L. Warren, W. M., of Rising Star Lodge, No. 450, Yonkers, N. Y.]
* * * It is extremely gratifying to learn that you have been furnished with funds sufficient to meet the extraordinary demands for relief occasioned by the unprecedented calamity to your city, and that a surplus still remains to be returned to the donors ; a state of affairs creditable alike to the liberality with which the fraternity responded to the appeal of their suffering Brethren in Chicago, and to the judgment and discrimination of your Board in distributing the funds. * * *

[From Wm. T. Lloyd, W. M., of Merchants Lodge, No. 709, New York.]
* * * Fully appreciating the motive which has prompted the return of the amount, beg you to accept the thanks of my Lodge for same, in the hope and belief that the suffering consequent upon the disaster referred to, has, under your auspices, been thoroughly alleviated. * * *

[From Jos. Eichbaum, Secretary of St. John's Lodge, No. 219, Pittsburg, Pa.]
* * * It is gratifying to know that the calls for aid for your distressed were liberally responded to, and if you got too much, we certainly cannot object to a return of the surplus, as the poor are always with us. * * *

[From F. T. Headley, Secretary of Bunker Hill Lodge, No. 151, Illinois.]
* * * Permit this Lodge to bear witness to the high degree of Masonic integrity exhibited by your committee in this transaction. * * *

MASONIC BOARD OF RELIEF. 157

[From E. C. Neall, Secretary of Chesterfield Lodge, No. 445, Illinois.]
* * * Reposing full trust and confidence in your committee, and believing that they have left no duties undischarged. * * *

[From R. Mendenhall, W. M., of Dallas City Lodge, No. 235, Illinois.]
* * * Duly appreciating your economical distribution of the fund. *

[From John D. Crabtree, W. M., of Friendship Lodge, No. 7. Dixon, Illinois.]
* * * On behalf of my Lodge, I tender you my sincere thanks and congratulations for the able and faithful discharge of the duties devolved upon you as President of the Board. * * *

ACKNOWLEDGMENTS.

Of the receipts of the surplus returned, have also been received from the following named parties:

Hon. Leonidas E. Pratt, Grand Master of California.
Hon. Chas. F. Stansbury, Grand Master of the District of Columbia.
Hon. E. B. Jones, Grand Master of Kentucky.
Hon. Christian Fetta, Grand Master of Indiana.
Hon. John W. Simonds, in behalf of the donors in Central America.
Benj. F. Underhill, Sec'y of United Brethren Lodge, Marlboro', Mass.
Ivory H. Pope, Sec'y of Jos. Warren Lodge, Boston, Mass.
Geo. Lee, W. M. of La Fayette Lodge, No. 100, Hartford, Conn.
James Scrimgeour, W. M. of Greenwood Lodge, No. 569, Brooklyn, N.Y.
T. Gayley, P. M. Shekinah Lodge, No. 246, Philadelphia, Pa.
D. L. Dunham, Sec'y Kankakee Lodge, No. 389, Ill.
S. R. Apperson, P. M. of Louisville Lodge, No. 196, Ill.
J. H. Megguire, W. M. of Chatsworth Lodge, No. 539, Ill.
Morris R. Locke, Sec'y of Jerseyville Lodge, No. 394, Ill.
Thomas A. Ray, Sec'y of Virden Lodge, No. 161, Ill.
Wm. H. Fairclough, Sec'y of Doric Lodge, No. 319, Moline, Ill.

SUPPLEMENTAL CASH ACCOUNT.

D. C. CREGIER,
              To MASONIC BOARD OF RELIEF, *Dr.*

1872.
Sept. 2. To Cash, as per Recording Secretary's Cash Account, ----------$1,394 57
Nov. 15. " " premium on Gold Drafts, and Interest on Deposits in Bank, etc.,---- 153 90
                                                                     ————$1,548 47

————*Cr.*————

Sept. 19. By Cash, for expenses of Auditing Commission,--------------------$ 401 49
Oct. 19. " " for H. Duvall, services,---------- 50 00
Nov. 15. " " for Hazlitt & Reed, for printing and binding 2,000 copies of this Report, as per contract,---------- 906 00
" " " " for Postage and Express Charges on 1,200 copies of this Report to Donors,---------------------- 180 00
" " " " for Permanent Masonic Board of Relief,------------------------ 10 98
                                                  ————$ 1,548 47

Vouchers on file.

NOTICE TO DONORS.

A copy of this Report has been sent, either by mail or express, to each donor; that is to say, to each contributing Lodge, Chapter, Commandery and individual; addressed to the Secretary of the body, or the individual it is intended for.

Those due in New York City and Brooklyn were sent to James M. Austin, M. D., Grand Secretary of N. Y. Those for Philadelphia to John Thomson, Grand Secretary of Pa. Those for Boston, South Boston and Boston Highlands, to Charles H. Titus, Grand Secretary of Mass. The officers of Lodges in the above named cities are requested to call on their Grand Secretaries for the Reports.

The contributions are credited, first under the name of State, next under the name of the city or town, alphabetically arranged, and directly to the party making the donation; the name of person or committee forwarding same is also given.

Please acknowledge receipt of the Report, care P. O. Box 375, Chicago, Ill.

Fraternally,

Recording Secretary.

CONTENTS.

List of Lodges Burned Out	3
List of Chapters Burned Out	4
List of Commanderies Burned Out	4
List of A. A. Scottish Rite Bodies Burned Out	4
Temporary Organization of Relief Committee	4
Organization of Board	5–6
Officers of Board	5–6
Donors, Instructions of	7
Rail Road Donations	9, 71
President's Report	10–30
Surplus Returned	11–13, 22–24, 103–107
Allotment to Chicago Lodges	17
Special Report of Board	30–33
Report of Auditing Commission	36–43
Donors, List of	44–92
Account of Disbursements	93–107
General Cash Account	108
Recording Secretary's Cash Account	108, 109, 137
Treasurer's Report	110
Statement of Distributions	111–137
Appeals for Aid	139–147
Acknowledgement of Receipt of Surplus Returned	148–157
Supplemental Cash Account	158
Notice to Donors	159

www.ingramcontent.com/pod-product-compliance
Lightning Source LLC
Chambersburg PA
CBHW022120160426
43197CB00009B/1098